Study Guide

for

Spielvogel's

Western Civilization

Sixth Edition

Volume II: Since 1500

James T. Baker
Western Kentucky University

THOMSON

WADSWORTH

Australia • Canada • Mexico • Singapore • Spain • United Kingdom • United States

Printed in the United States of America
2 3 4 5 6 7 09 08 07 06

Printer: Thomson West

ISBN 0-495-03091-0

Thomson Higher Education
10 Davis Drive
Belmont, CA 94002-3098
USA

Asia (including India)
Thomson Learning
5 Shenton Way
#01-01 UIC Building
Singapore 068808

Australia/New Zealand
Thomson Learning Australia
102 Dodds Street
Southbank, Victoria 3006
Australia

Canada
Thomson Nelson
1120 Birchmount Road
Toronto, Ontario M1K 5G4
Canada

UK/Europe/Middle East/Africa
Thomson Learning
High Holborn House
50–51 Bedford Road
London WC1R 4LR
United Kingdom

Latin America
Thomson Learning
Seneca, 53
Colonia Polanco
11560 Mexico
D.F. Mexico

Spain (including Portugal)
Thomson Paraninfo
Calle Magallanes, 25
28015 Madrid, Spain

CONTENTS

PREFACE

This study guide is designed to accompany the text *Western Civilization* by Jackson J. Spielvogel. It contains nine types of exercises.

1. Learning Objectives—major points that you may read before you begin the chapter and use to test your knowledge when you have finished.
2. Glossary of Terms—important names, places, ideas, and works of literature, art, and music to know before you begin the chapter.
3. Words to Match with Their Definitions—important terms to be matched with their meanings; a second form of identification.
4. Multiple Choice Questions—20 questions for each chapter; a way of testing factual and conceptual learning.
5. Sentences to Complete—blank spaces are provided for you to complete an interpretive statement with specific words and phrases.
6. Chronological Arrangement— a set of seven events for each chapter that you give dates for and place in chronological order.
7. Questions for Critical Thought—questions that encourage you to recall and relate important concepts and prepare you for essay examinations.
8. Analysis of Primary Source Documents—questions that help you consider and discuss the primary documents found in the boxes of each chapter.
9. Map Exercises—exercises to test your knowledge of geographical regions and specific places important to the historical period.

You will probably be asked on your examinations to write essays. Essays not only test your knowledge of the facts, but your ability to interpret and apply them. In this volume, Questions for Critical Thought and Analysis of Primary Source Documents should be of help to you in preparing for essay questions. In addition, let me offer you several suggestions on how to write essays that will both teach you and help you make high marks:

1. Read the entire question, and be sure that you understand exactly what is being asked and that you consider all parts of it. Address yourself only to the question that is asked, but address yourself to every section of it.
2. Make an outline before you begin to write the essay. Jot down in as few words as possible the major points you want to make, and the most important persons, places, and ideas you want to include. Glance back at your outline as you write so that you will not stay too long on one point or omit another.
3. Try to make one major point in your essay, with all of the others subordinate to it. This is your thesis. State it at the beginning, refer back to it at various appropriate times, and restate it briefly at the end. This will keep you focused on a unifying theme.
4. Write for an imaginary reader who is intelligent but does not necessarily know the information you are relating. This way you will not fail to provide all information necessary to explain yourself, but you will also not insult your reader.

5. Be careful to spell correctly and to use good grammar. A history course is not an English course, and graders may or may not "count off" for poor spelling and grammar; but all graders are impressed either positively or negatively by the quality of your mechanics. While you may not see a specific comment about such matters on your essay, you may be sure that they have affected your final grade.

6. Think of an essay in a positive light. It should and can be an exercise in which the facts you have learned take focus and shape and make more sense than ever before. If done correctly, an essay can be the truest learning experience you can have and the most certain measure of your achievement.

I hope that this booklet adds to your enjoyment of the study of Western Civilization, increases your understanding of the ages you study, and helps you achieve high marks.

James T. Baker

Study Guide

for

Spielvogel's

Western Civilization
Sixth Edition

Volume II: Since 1500

CHAPTER THIRTEEN
REFORMATION AND RELIGIOUS WARFARE IN THE SIXTEENTH CENTURY

Chapter Outline

I. Prelude to Reformation
   A. Christian (or Northern Renaissance) Humanism
      1. Focus on Religious Simplicity
      2. Call for Religious Reform
      3. Reform through Education
   B. Erasmus: Prince of Humanists
      1. Emphasis on Inner Piety
      2. *Praise of Folly*: Satire of the Age
      3. Influence on the Protestant Revolt
   C. Thomas More: Christian Conscience of His Age
      1. *Utopia*: Blueprint for a More Perfect Society
      2. Henry VIII and the Royal Divorce

II. Church and Religion on the Eve of the Reformation
   A. Abuses of the Clergy: Pluralism, Absenteeism
   B. Popular Religion
      1. Passion for Relics
      2. Thomas à Kempis' *Imitation of Christ*
      3. Indulgences

III. Martin Luther and the Reformation in Germany
   A. Early Luther
      1. From the Peasantry
      1. From Law to the Monastery
      2. "Justification by Grace through Faith"
      3. Attack on the Sale of Indulgences
      4. Trial at Worms
   B. Development of Lutheranism
      1. Urban Phenomenon
      2. Philip Melanchthon as Theologian
      3. Support for Authority against the Peasants
      4. Union of Church and State: National Churches

IV. Germany and the Reformation: Religion and Politics
   A. Emperor Charles V's Attempt to Preserve Christian Unity
   B. Schmalkaldic (Lutheran) League
   C. Peace of Augsburg: Success of Lutheranism

V. Spread of the Protestant Reformation
   A. Lutheranism's Success in Scandinavia
   B. Ulrich Zwingli's Failure in Switzerland

    C. Radical Reformation: Anabaptists
        1. Church as a Body of Believers
        2. Lord's Supper as Symbolic Remembrance
        3. Separation of Church and State
        4. Fiasco at Münster
        5. Menno Simons and the Mennonites
    D. Reformation in England
        1. King Henry's Divorce and Separation from Rome
        2. Edward VI and a More Protestant Church
        3. Mary's Attempt to Restore Catholicism
    E. Calvinism
        1. John Calvin's *Institutes of the Christian Religion*
        2. Doctrine of Predestination
        3. Calvin's Geneva and the Spread of Calvinism

VI. Social Impact of the Reformation
    A. Effect on Families
        1. More Positive Attitudes
        2. Place of Women
        3. Home Devotions
    B. Education in the Reformation
        1. Rise of the German Gymnasium
        2. Genevan Academy
    C. Religious Practices and Popular Culture
        1. Decline of "Catholic" Practices Among Protestants
        2. Reform of Social Practices and the Rise of Puritanism

VII. Catholic Reformation
    A. New Mysticism: Teresa of Avila
    B. Regeneration of Religious Orders
    C. Rise of New Orders
        1. Theatines
        2. Oratory of Divine Love
        3. Society of Jesus
            a. Ignatius Loyola
            b. Missionaries Francis Xavier and Matteo Ricci
    D. Revived Papacy
        1. Paul III and the Council of Trent
        2. Paul IV and the Index
    E. Council of Trent
        1. Reform of the Catholic Church
        2. Clear Body of Doctrine

VIII. Politics and Wars of Religion in the Sixteenth Century
    A. French Wars of Religion (1562-1598)
        1. Catholics and Huguenots
        2. War of the Three Henries (1588-1589)
        3. Henry IV's Conversion and the Edict of Nantes

B. Philip II and Militant Catholicism
1. "Most Catholic King"
2. Leader of the Holy League
3. William of Orange and Dutch Independence
C. England of Elizabeth
1. Acts of Supremacy and Uniformity
2. Mary Queen of Scots
3. Spanish Armada

Chapter Summary

The great religious earthquake called the Reformation, which split the church into two and then into a dozen parts, was caused by a variety of social and economic developments. Still it depended upon the Renaissance humanism of its day for an intellectual rationale. Christian humanists, particularly in the north of Europe, led the movement to reform and purify the Catholic Church, even though some of them refused to be Protestants; and it was their writings which gave the Reformation its direction.

The Reformation began with Martin Luther's criticism of the sale of indulgences and his subsequent excommunication. It spread from Germany to Switzerland through the work of John Calvin and Ulrich Zwingli and to Scotland and Holland through the work of Calvin's disciples. Although in England the break with the Catholic Church came because Henry VIII wanted a divorce, the English Reformation grew more radical after Henry's death. Christendom fragmented.

While northern Europe, with the notable exceptions of France, Poland, and Ireland, left the Catholic faith, the southern nations of Italy, Spain, and Portugal, as well as France and Austria, remained firmly Catholic. The Council of Trent, called too late to stop the permanent division, confirmed the Catholic teachings of the Middle Ages while implementing many of the reforms of practice advocated by Luther and Calvin. The Age of Reformation left all of the churches stronger in conviction yet at war with each other over authority.

In France the Catholic establishment tried to wipe out the Protestant minority, the Huguenots, and came to an uneasy peace only with the Edict of Nantes. Philip II, who earned the title "Most Catholic King," blocked all Protestant activity in his Spanish kingdom but lost his Dutch provinces to the Protestant House of Orange and his naval Armada to Protestant England. The English queen Elizabeth presided over the establishment of a national church that included most Englishmen but did not tolerate those who chose a different path.

The modern world began with violent disputes about the will of God.

Learning Objectives

1. Be able to describe the status and character of the Catholic Church just prior to the outbreak of the Reformation, and show how such things contributed to the breakup of Christianity.

2. Outline the major points of contention between Martin Luther and the Church, and show why they did not find a way to compromise and avoid schism.

3. Discuss the various forms Protestantism took and how these groups became dominant in various parts of Europe.

4. Examine the social and economic impact of the Reformation and Protestantism on the continent of Europe.

5. Describe the Catholic Reformation, show how it responded to Protestant criticism, and how it created the modern Catholic Church.

Glossary of Names and Terms

1. Thomas à Kempis: author of *The Imitation of Christ*, an example of the Catholic movement toward pietism and mysticism just before the Reformation.

2. Wittenberg: German city where Martin Luther posted his *Ninety-five Theses*, which precipitated the Protestant Reformation.

3. Edict of Worms: imperial decree branding Luther a criminal and ordering that his books be burned as heresy.

4. Katharina von Bora: former nun whom Luther married, providing a model for the Protestant ministry of the future.

5. Thomas More: former Lord Chancellor of England who supported the pope's refusal to grant Henry VIII a divorce and was beheaded as a traitor.

6. Calvinism: the form of Protestantism originated and led by John Calvin, centered at Geneva, which spread more widely than any other branch of the movement.

7. Society of Jesus: founded by Ignatius of Loyola, this religious order became the most powerful instrument of the Catholic Reformation.

8. Council of Trent: meeting of Catholic leaders from 1545 to 1563 which dealt with abuses and created the modern Church.

9. Edict of Nantes: decree from King Henry IV that established Catholicism as the official religion of France but gave freedom of worship to Huguenots.

10. Act of Uniformity: made the Book of Common Prayer standard for worship in England and essentially established the Protestant Church of England.

Match the Following Words with their Definitions:

1.	Johann Eck	A.	Nun who married Martin Luther
2.	Philip Melanchthon	B.	Henry VIII's second wife
3.	Katharina von Bora	C.	Pacifist leader of Dutch Anabaptists
4.	Ulrich Zwingli	D.	City declared by radical Anabaptists to be the New Jerusalem
5.	Munster	E.	Huguenot who became a Catholic to gain a crown
6.	Menno Simons	F.	Luther's opponent in the Leipzig debate
7.	Thomas Cranmer	G.	Jesuit missionary to India and Japan
8.	Anne Boleyn	H.	Archbishop of Canterbury who granted Henry VIII's divorce
9.	Francis Xavier	I.	Lutheran scholar who became known as "Teacher of Germany"
10.	Henry IV	J.	Leader of the Swiss Reformed Church movement

Choose the Correct Answer:

1. The Christian humanists were

    a. pessimistic about the future of humanity.
    b. realistic about their dreams for the church.
    c. supported by wealthy German patrons.
    d. doubtful about the benefits of education.
    e. frequently on the run from the law.

2. Erasmus hoped to reform Christianity through all of the following *except*

    a. spreading the radical reform ideas of Luther.
    b. ridiculing the abuses of the church.
    c. providing readers a New Testament in the original Greek.
    d. teaching the "philosophy of Christ" as a guide for daily life.
    e. showing people how to return to the simplicity of the early church.

3. In his book *Utopia*, Thomas More

    a. argued that Christians could not be humanists.
    b. heralded the coming of Martin Luther.
    c. outlined a harmonious social order with communal property.
    d. argued that Henry VIII was wrong to want a divorce.
    e. defended the rights of the Huguenots.

4. Popular religion in the late Middle Ages and Renaissance witnessed a

    a. revival of mysticism called the Modern Devotion.
    b. decline in interest in sacred relics.
    c. decline in the sale of indulgences for remission of sins.
    d. careful and comprehensive reform of church practices.
    e. demanded that kings revive the Crusades.

5. Martin Luther's early monastic life was characterized by

    a. a tendency to forget his daily ritual duties.
    b. an obsession with his own sinfulness.
    c. his devotion to the study of canon law.
    d. rejection of the Bible as the Word of God.
    e. occasional dalliance with local women.

6. Luther finally answered the question "How can I be saved?" by

    a. the doctrine of justification by grace through faith.
    b. doing good works aimed at achieving universal brotherhood.
    c. following the Rule of the Augustinian Order.
    d. taking the sacraments every day.
    e. leaving monastic life to marry and have children.

7. Luther and Zwingli parted company over the issue of the

    a. separation of church and state.
    b. ordination and priesthood of women.
    c. use of musical instruments in the church.
    d. doctrine of the Lord's Supper.
    e. whether ministers should marry.

8. The Edict of Worms

    a. included Luther's statement "Here I stand."
    b. expressed Luther's feelings about the authority of Leo X.
    c. called on Luther to appear before Charles V to recant his heresies.
    d. protected Luther so long as he remained in Saxony.
    e. made Luther an outlaw within the Holy Roman Empire.

9. The Peasants' War of 1524-1525 was

    a. inspired by the writings of Lutheran theologian Philip Melanchthon.
    b. one reason Lutheranism spread so quickly throughout Europe.
    c. applauded by Luther for helping bring down Catholicism.
    d. a revolt by people of rising expectations against their local lords.
    e. instrumental in making Henry IV King of France.

10. The Swiss leader Zwingli

    a. instituted his reforms after a military coup in Zurich.
    b. favored elaborate church ceremonies on Christmas and Easter.
    c. stressed the need for state supervision over the church.
    d. preserved remnants of papal Christianity such as confession.
    e. was condemned to death by the Calvinist Consistory.

11. The immediate cause of the English Reformation was

    a. continual papal interference in affairs of state.
    b. the influence of Luther's life and writings in England.
    c. Cardinal Wolsey's plot against Henry VIII.
    d. Queen Catherine's failure to produce a male heir.
    e. Thomas More's weak defense of papal authority.

12. Find the *false* description among the following officials of Henry VIII.

    a. Thomas More—Lord Chancellor executed for not accepting King Henry's authority over the church.
    b. Thomas Cranmer—Archbishop of Canterbury executed for refusing to annul the king's marriage.
    c. Thomas Cromwell—principal secretary who confiscated monasteries to bolster the treasury without royal authority.
    d. Cardinal Wolsey—Lord Chancellor who tried but failed to gain a papal annulment of the king's marriage.
    e. Clement VII—Medici pope who found it politically impossible to grant Henry's petition for divorce.

13. The reign of England's Queen Mary I was noted for

   a.   her failure to restore Catholicism.
   b.   constant warfare with her Spanish territories.
   c.   an end to the English Reformation.
   d.   her Act of Supremacy in 1534.
   e.   the heir she produced after she was 40.

14. Which of the following statements best describes the reform movement of John Calvin?

   a.   Its rejection of Luther's doctrine of "justification by faith alone" gave it a Catholic tone.
   b.   Its doctrine of Predestination made it essentially a passive faith.
   c.   Its belief that men must "obey God rather than man" made Calvinists willing to rebel against secular power.
   d.   Its conviction that God watches man's deeds kept it from interfering in people's private lives.
   e.   Its mysticism made it grant individual members the right to interpret the Bible as their "inner light" directed them.

15. Calvin's doctrine of Predestination

   a.   taught that material wealth was a sign of being one of the elect.
   b.   made Calvinists more certain than other Christians that they were doing God's will on earth.
   c.   assumed that God had predestined the male to be the head of the family and society.
   d.   was within his lifetime added to most Protestant confessions of faith.
   e.   never caught on with his followers and was abandoned after his death.

16. Typically in Protestant societies

   a.   women were encouraged to pursue public careers.
   b.   women were restricted to the roles of wife and mother.
   c.   the celibate life was considered superior to marriage.
   d.   children were never physically punished.
   e.   no child remained at home after age 18.

17. Protestant educators

   a.   retained humanist principles of pedagogy and curriculum.
   b.   attempted to educate as large a percentage of the population as possible.
   c.   sought to produce both good pastors and good state servants.
   d.   divided students into classes based on age and capabilities.
   e.   did all of the above.

18. At the Council of Trent, the Catholic Church

   a.   established a clear body of doctrine under a supreme pontiff.
   b.   upheld the right, under certain circumstances, of the church to sell indulgences.
   c.   reaffirmed the doctrine of Purgatory but made no statement about Transubstantiation.
   d.   established the authority for doctrine on tradition above scripture.
   e.   made clerical celibacy a personal choice.

19. In France just prior to the Wars of Religion there

   a. the nobility was between 40and 50 percent Huguenot.
   b. the general population was evenly split between Huguenots and Catholics.
   c. Catherine de Medici's succeeded in suppressing most Protestant dissent.
   d. a wealthy Catholic majority lorded over a poverty stricken Huguenot minority.
   e. John Calvin made a triumphal tour, converting many Catholics.

20. The French Wars of Religion (1562-1598)

   a. ended when the Huguenots won a decisive battle in the field.
   b. ended when Henry IV guaranteed rights both to Catholics and Huguenots.
   c. ended on Saint Bartholomew's Day with a Huguenot massacre.
   d. were entire a French affair, without ties to conflicts elsewhere.
   e. ended only when Louis XIV banished all Protestants from France.

Complete the Following Sentences:

1. Thomas More's ideal society, outlined in his book _____, was not at all like the real world where he died because he would not approve the _____ of King _____.

2. Martin Luther, an _____ monk, criticized the sales of _____ in his famous _____ Theses.

3. In the greatest social upheaval of his lifetime, the Peasants War, Luther sided with the German _____ against the German _____. Order was necessary, he argued, for the spread of the _____.

4. Ulrich Zwingli ultimately failed in his attempt to unite the reformed churches of _____ and _____ when he and Luther could not agree on the meaning of the _____ _____.

5. The Anabaptist movement got a bad image when a radical group called _____ set up their "Kingdom of God" at the German city of _____, calling it the _____ _____.

6. Thomas Cranmer helped Henry VIII divorce Queen _____ and marry _____ _____, then moved England toward Protestantism under Henry's heir, _____.

7. John Calvin's emphasis in his great book, _____ ____ ____ _____ _____, was on the absolute _____ of God, which led him to defend the doctrine of _____.

8. Protestantism took away women's religious profession, the life of a nun, and said they must be only _____ and _____ , a "gladsome" punishment for the sin of _____.

9. Henry of Navarre left the _____ faith to become a _____ in order to gain the throne of _____.

10. When convinced that _____ planned to depose her in favor of her cousin _____, Queen Elizabeth of England had her rival _____.

Place the Following in Chronological Order and Give Dates:

1. Society of Jesus recognized   1.

2. English Act of Supremacy   2.

3. Council of Trent convenes   3.

4. Diet of Worms   4.

5. Destruction of the Spanish Armada   5.

6. John Calvin publishes his *Institutes*   6.

7. Schmalkaldic League formed   7.

Questions for Critical Thought

1. Describe northern Renaissance humanism, and show how it differed from that of its earlier form in Italy.

2. What conditions in the Church of the early sixteenth century made the Reformation both possible and probable? What part did Erasmus play in pointing them out?

3. Describe Martin Luther's part in the Protestant revolt. What personal qualities made Luther act as he did, and how did his actions affect the course of the Reformation?

4. Explain how the Anabaptists differed from the Lutherans. Why did even Protestants such as Luther despise and fear them?

5. Discuss the Reformation in England. What caused it? How did it differ from the Reformation in other places? What were its results?

6. Describe the work of John Calvin and the development of Calvinism? Explain why and how he came to have such widespread influence in Protestantism?

7. What shape did the Catholic Reformation take? How did the reformed Catholic Church differ from Protestantism? How well did its reforms prepare it for future ages?

8. Why were the various wars of religion across the continent of Europe so bloody? Why did the participants emphasize their differences and fight so hard to suppress opposition?

Analysis of Primary Source Documents

1. What did Erasmus find ridiculous about the monastic life of his day? Describe his sense of humor.

2. Why did Martin Luther's classroom exercise, The Ninety-Five Theses, cause such a sensation and have such an impact on his society and times.

3. Compare and contrast the Luther who was a rebel against ecclesiastical authority with the Luther who wrote the treatise against the peasants. How do you account for the differences?

4. Using the Marburg Colloquy as your guide, draw as many conclusions as you can about Luther's personality, mind, and public manner.

5. To what degree did John Calvin's Genevan Consistory control the personal lives of citizens? Give examples. What sort of city did this create?

6. If Katherine Zell is typical of the Anabaptist faith, what new themes did this movement bring to Christianity? To what extent were these themes the natural consequences of Luther's doctrinal innovations?

7. If one follows Loyola's formula for correct Christian thinking, what does the Christian believe? How does the Christian act? What does the Christian accomplish?

8. How does Queen Elizabeth's speech before Parliament in 1601 demonstrate her political acumen? To what extent did being an unmarried woman add to the image she adopted as her public *persona*?

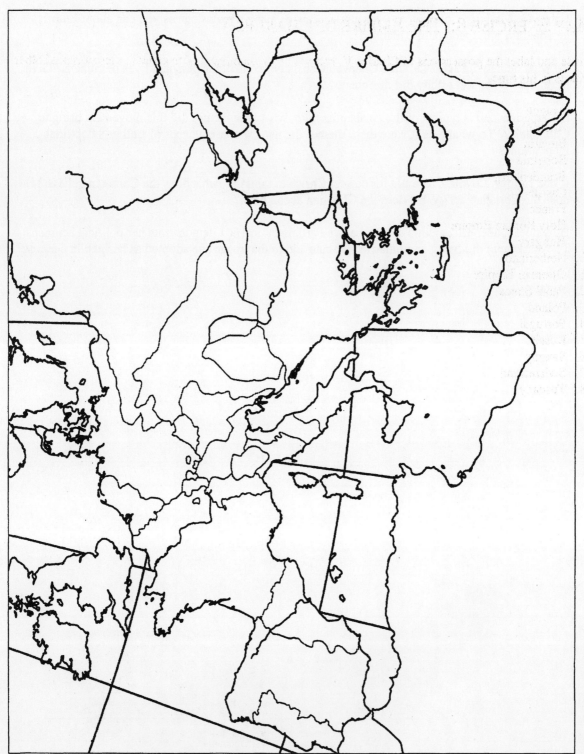

Map Exercise 8

MAP EXERCISE 8: THE EMPIRE OF CHARLES V

Shade and label the possessions of Charles V, and with various other shades show the territories of other princes in his time.

1. Aragon
2. Austria
3. Bavaria
4. Bohemia
5. Brandenburg
6. Castile
7. France
8. Holy Roman Empire
9. Hungary
10. Netherlands
11. Ottoman Empire
12. Papal States
13. Poland
14. Portugal
15. Russia
16. Saxony
17. Switzerland
18. Tuscany

CHAPTER FOURTEEN
EUROPE AND THE WORLD:
NEW ENCOUNTERS, 1500-1800

Chapter Outline

I.   On the Brink of a New World
     A. Motives for European Exploration
         1. Fascination with the East
         2. Wealth through Trade
         3. Christian Missions
     B. Technological Means Needed

II. New Horizons: Portuguese and Spanish Empires
     A. Portuguese Maritime Empire
         1. Prince Henry, the Navigator
         2. Bartholomew Dias around the Cape
         3. Vasco da Gama to India
         4. China
     B. Voyages to the New World
         1. Christopher Columbus
         2. John Cabot
         3. Balboa and Magellan
         4. Treaty of Tordesillas
     C. Spanish Empire in the New World
         1. Early Civilizations in Mesoamerica
         2. Spanish Conquest of the Aztec Empire
         3. Hernán Cortés and Mexico
         4. Francisco Pizarro and Peru
         5. Administration

III. New Rivals Enter the Scene: Dutch, British, and French
     A. African Slave Trade
         1. Growth of the Slave Trade
         2. Effects and End of Slave Trade
     B. West in Southeast Asia
     C. French and British in India
     D. China
     E. Japan
     F. Americas
         1. West Indies
         2. North America

IV. Toward a World Economy
     A. Economic Conditions in the Sixteenth Century
     B. Growth of Commercial Capitalism
     C. Mercantilism
     D. Overseas Trade and Colonies: A Global Economy?

V.   Impact of European Expansion
     Conquered
     Conquerors

Chapter Summary

The energies released by the Renaissance and the rivalries unleashed by the Reformation made the sixteenth and seventeenth centuries an era of discovery, expansion, and commerce.
It was an age of danger, opportunity, and achievement.

Long fascinated by the world beyond their shores, Europeans in the late fifteenth century had the technological skills finally to go exploring; and what they found expanded both their minds and their treasuries. First the Portuguese and Spanish, then the Dutch, English, and French sent out expeditions that resulted in empires in the "New World" discovered by Columbus and in the older world of Asia. Between 1500 and 1800 European came to dominate, both culturally and economically, much of the known world.

With ships linking far-flung empires, the world of commercial capitalism was born. Nations attempted to enrich themselves through centrally controlled systems of mercantilism; but their efforts proved only partially successful. Mercantilism was doomed ultimately to failure as the first global economy, with multiple interdependencies evolved.

The discoveries, conquests, and organization of empires did not come freely. Native peoples were subjugated and enslaved; natural resources were depleted; and the conquerors each year were more convinced of the superiority of their culture and race. The twenty-first century is surrounded by the structures and rubble of Europe's first encounter with the rest of the world.

Learning Objectives

1.   Be able to explain the motives that fueled Europe's early modern overseas exploration and expansion and the new technologies that made it possible.

2.   Describe the way the Portuguese were able to establish an overseas empire and the way it functioned.

3.   Describe the creation and characteristics of the Spanish Empire in the Americas.

4.   Discuss the economic philosophies that dominated Europe and the way they affected the world economy Europeans established.

5.   Explain the religious, social, and economic effects of European conquests around the globe on both the conquerors and those they conquered.

Glossary of Names and Terms

1.   John Mandeville: author of a book of fantasy literature about the wonders of the world beyond Europe, the inspiration for many foreign voyages.

2.   Henry the Navigator: member of the Portuguese royal family who founded a school for navigators and encouraged exploration down the west coast of Africa.

3.   Columbus: attempted to reach Asia by sailing west into the Atlantic and in the process landed in a "new world."

4. Tordesillas: a city on the border of Spain and Portugal where a treaty dividing the pagan world between the two countries was blessed by the pope.

5. *Encomienda*: Spanish royal system which allowed conquerors to use Indians as labor but required that they convert them to Christianity and protect them from abuse.

6. De las Casas: Dominican friar whose writings exposed the cruelty of the Spanish against the Indians and led to reforms in the imperial system.

7. Dutch East India Company: financial organization that made huge profits in the Indonesian archipelago and set the stage for the creation of the Dutch Empire there.

8. Robert Clive: British military commander who established his country's supremacy over both native rulers and other Europeans powers in India.

9. Samuel de Champlain: founder of the first French settlement in North America, at Quebec, which set the stage for the establishment of New France.

10. Mercantilism: the dominant economic theory of early modern Europe, which assumed that the total volume of trade was unchangeable and that each country must gain and keep as large a percentage of it as possible.

Match the Following Words with their Definitions:

1.	Prester John	A.	Person of mixed European and African bloodlines
2.	Albuquerque	B.	Mythical figure that inspired Portuguese exploration to the east
3.	Ferdinand Magellan	C.	Agreement which divided non-Christian lands between Spain and Portugal
4.	Treaty of Tordesillas		
5.	Francesco Pizarro	D.	Person of mixed European and Indian bloodlines
6.	Plassey	E.	Spanish explorer whose expedition was the first to circumnavigate the earth
7.	Champlain	F.	Established the first French settlement in Canada
8.	Mestizo	G.	Naval cartographer
9.	Mulatto	H.	Sit of British victory over Mughals
10.	Gerardus Mercator	I.	Spanish general who conquered the Incan Empire
		J.	Established Portuguese trading post of Goa

Choose the Correct Answer:

1. Portuguese expansionism was inspired by

    a. missionary zeal to convert the lost peoples of the Americas.
    b. a desire to catch up with the Spanish.
    c. severe droughts that had left Portugal without an adequate food supply.
    d. strong support from members of the royal family.
    e. the preaching, throughout Portugal, of Prester John.

2. Spanish exploration of and expansion into the New World is best exemplified by

    a. Amerigo Vespucci's circumnavigation of the globe.
    b. Hernán Cortés' conquest of the Aztec Empire.
    c. Ferdinand Magellan's conquest of the Incas.
    d. Vasco da Gama's successes in Calicut.
    e. Francisco Pizarro's discovery of the Pacific Ocean.

3. The name America that was given to the New World came from Amerigo Vespucci,

    a. a Spanish pirate.
    b. an Italian writer.
    c. an Italian missionary.
    d. a Portuguese governmental official.
    e. the first governor of New Spain.

4. The Treaty of Tordesillas

    a. was forced on Spain by the pope.
    b. showed the rising international power of France.
    c. divided the non-European world between Portugal and Spain.
    d. ended the Thirty Years' War.
    e. had its greatest impact on North America.

5. Hernán Cortés was aided in his conquest of the Aztecs by

    a. Moctezuma's loss of self-confidence.
    b. other tribes hostile to the Aztecs.
    c. an outbreak of smallpox.
    d. Spanish certainty that they represented God.
    e. all of the above

6. The *encomienda* system

    a. exploited native Americans to enrich Spaniards.
    b. protected native Americans against capitalists.
    c. gave the Jesuits administrative control over the West Indies.
    d. failed to be approved in the Spanish *cortes.*
    e. was defended by de las Casas.

7. Bartolomé de las Casas, a Dominican monk, was known for his

    a. cruel and barbarous treatment of Indians.
    b. magnificent lifestyle on a Cuban plantation.
    c. revelations about the cruel treatment of Indians under Spanish rule.
    d. creation of the Native American Catholic church.
    e. translation of Native American poetry into English.

8. The Boers were

    a. German mercenaries who helped the Dutch establish colonies in India.
    b. Dutch farmers who settled in South Africa.
    c. an Order of Franciscan missionaries to China.
    d. Dutch businessmen who developed silver mines in South Africa.
    e. a destructive insect that destroyed many South American crops.

9. Trade in African slaves increased in the early sixteenth century because

    a. wealthy Europeans came to view them as symbols of wealth.
    b. victorious African tribes sought new markets for their conquered enemies.
    c. sugar production in the West Indies demanded ever more laborers.
    d. Africans were well suited by nature to work in the tropics.
    e. no one spoke out against the slave trade.

10. One effect of the slave trade on the African nation of Benin was an increase in

    a. the overall health of the population left behind.
    b. religious devotion to traditional gods.
    c. violent attacks on European diplomats.
    d. the practice of human sacrifice.
    e. the rise of a wealthy black middle class.

11. During the seventeenth century the Dutch replaced the Portuguese and English as

    a. chief merchants of the Asian spice trade.
    b. the most successful missionaries to Africa.
    c. colonial masters of southeast Asia.
    d. managers of the sugar plantations of the West Indies.
    e. the most powerful Protestant force in the world.

12. The effects of the Seven Years' War on India was

    a. an increase of Portuguese influence.
    b. the complete withdrawal of France.
    c. independence for the city-state of Calcutta.
    d. the establishment of the Anglican Church.
    e. severe famine and a decline in population.

13. In 1644 China was changed by a victory of the

    a. Manchus over the Ming dynasty.
    b. British over the French.
    c. Ming dynasty over Qing raiders.
    d. Great Kahn over British troops.
    e. Christian missionaries over Muslim rulers.

14. The Tokugawa rulers of Japan

    a. were Japan's first Christian dynasty.
    b. created the shogunate military code of conduct.
    c. established the longest ruling dynasty in Japanese history.
    d. built one of the world's largest navies..
    e. lasted only a few years, until the British mandate.

15. France lost its North American empire due in part to its inability to

    a. develop institutions that suited the harsh climate.
    b. produce capable military commanders.
    c. stave off Indian attacks.
    d. get more French settlers to emigrate to the New World.
    e. fight battles in cold weather.

16. The tie between European banking and the mining industry is best illustrated by

    a. Philip II's grant of gold mining rights in Peru to the Pizarro family.
    b. Charles I's grant of mining monopolies to Jacob Fugger.
    c. William of Orange's grant of monopolies in the Hudson Valley to the Bourse.
    d. James I's grant of monopolies to the London Company.
    e. Louis XIV's grant of monopolies in Quebec to Jacques Cartier.

17. Under the mercantile system, nations sought to increase their share of the

    a. world's gold and silver bullion holdings.
    b. number of slaves traded annually worldwide.
    c. small businesses within their countries.
    d. missionary responsibility for converting the pagans.
    e. logging and fur enterprises in North America.

18. Juana Inés de la Cruz advocated the

    a. erection of forts along the Saint Lawrence River.
    b. establishment of publishing houses to print Bibles in Native American languages.
    c. education of Native American women.
    d. equality of men and women in the New World.
    e. elevation of Mother Anna Matera to sainthood.

19. The Jesuits in Japan annulled their early missionary successes by

    a. encouraging rebellion against the imperial family.
    b. destroying native religious shrines.
    c. engaging in questionable business affairs.
    d. discouraging young men from becoming shogun soldiers.
    e. requiring converts to give up all but one of their wives.

20. The Mercator projection aided sea captains because it

    a. gave them a perfect picture of the earth's surface.
    b. allowed them to sail at night and in bad weather.
    c. cut through ice.
    d. provided them with true lines of direction.
    e. was available in all European languages.

Complete the Following Sentences:

1. Encouraged by the support of Prince Henry, known as the _____, Portuguese sailor _____ _____ _____ found a sea route to India, where Alfonso _____ _____ established an outpost that started an empire of trade.

2. In the Americas, Spaniard _____ _____ conquered the Aztecs, while _____ _____ conquered the Incas. Spanish treatment of Native Americans was later publicized by the monk Bartolomé _____ _____ _____.

3. The *encomienda* system permitted the Spanish to use Native Americans as _____ but also required them to _____ them and see to their _____ needs.

4. African slaves were packed into cargo ships _____ to _____ per ship for voyages that took as least _____ day, during which time an average of _____ % of them died.

5. Sir Robert Clive began the British consolidation of power in _____ when his army of _____ defeated a much larger Mughal-led army at _____.

6. In 1793 Britain's Lord _____ pressed the Chinese government to open cities other than _____ for foreign trade; but he was rebuffed by Emperor _____.

7. Japanese fears of foreign influence led first to their expulsion of _____ and then to the regulation that Dutch traders could visit only the port of _____ for no more than _____ months per year.

8. The thirteen British North American colonies had their own _____; and their merchants _____ and _____ all British attempts at colonial regulation.

9. The mercantile system assumed that the volume of trade was _____ and that economic activity was a form of _____ to determine which nations would prosper at the _____ of others.

10. The way European expansion affected the ecology of conquered lands is demonstrated by the introduction of beef _____ into the Americas, _____ _____ into the West Indies, and American _____ into Africa.

Place the Following in Chronological Order and Give Dates:

1. First African slaves arrive in America   1.

2. Battle of Plassey   2.

3. French cede Canada to Britain   3.

4. Treaty of Tordesillas   4.

5. Champlain establishes settlement in Quebec   5.

6. Dutch seize Malacca   6.

7. Dias rounds the point of Africa   7.

Questions for Critical Thought

1. Discuss the factors that encouraged and enabled Europeans to enter their period of expansion around the globe in the sixteenth century.

2. Describe the empire which the Spanish established in the Americas: its government, its social and religious systems, its economy, its strengths and weaknesses.

3. Describe and explain the rise of the African slave trade: causes, objectives, and results for the Americas.

4. Discuss the first European attempts to create spheres of influence in Asia. Why did they succeed in some places and fail in others?

5. Compare the British and French colonies in North America. What accounts for the British success and the French failure?

6. Describe the development of commercial capitalism in the seventeenth and eighteenth centuries. How did Europe become the world's most prosperous region?

7. Was the economy of the eighteenth century truly "global" in the contemporary sense? Explain why you think it was or was not.

8. Explain the effects European colonization of the Americas and some of Asia had on the conquered people and their conquerors.

Analysis of Primary Source Documents

1. How does Albuquerque's rationale for the conquest of Malacca demonstrate his loyalty to his two lords, God and the king? How is he able to make the two loyalties agree?

2. What did Columbus see as his two purposes in making the land he discovered a part of the Spanish Empire? Why did he believe this would easily be accomplished?

3. What did Cortes think of the Aztec civilization he conquered? What does he indicate made him feel justified in destroying it? What does this say about his own Spanish civilization?

4. Try to separate fact from fiction in de las Casas' account of the treatment of Native Americans by Spanish conquistadors. Is there enough fact and is it serious enough to cause a conscientious Spanish official to order changes? If so, how would you suggest he start?

5. What characteristics of the African slave trade did the Frenchman you have read find odious? How would a slave trader likely have justified his work against such criticism?

6. What assumptions lie behind Louis XIV's letter to the King of Tonkin? How was the king able to respond to Louis with dignity but without giving offense?

7. How did the Chinese emperor's reply to Lord Macartney differ from Tonkin's reply to Louis? What does this reply say about Chinese attitudes toward foreigners?

8. What kind of social and economic system did the Jesuits establish in southern South America? What did Felix de Azara find objectionable about it all?

Map Exercise 9

MAP EXERCISE 9: EUROPEAN OVERSEAS POSSESSIONS IN 1658

Shade and label the following:

1. Angola
2. Brazil
3. Caribbean Sea
4. India
5. Indian Ocean
6. Indonesia
7. Mozambique
8. New Spain
9. Peru
10. Philippines
11. Portugal
12. Spain

Pinpoint and label the following:

1. Calicut
2. Canton
3. Ceylon
4. Colombo
5. Goa
6. Lima
7. Macao
8. Tenochtitlán
9. Zanzibar

CHAPTER FIFTEEN

STATE BUILDING AND THE SEARCH FOR ORDER IN THE SEVENTEENTH CENTURY

Chapter Outline

I.   Social Crisis, War, and Rebellion
    A.   Witchcraft Craze
        1.   Religious Uncertainties
        2.   Social Change
    B.   Thirty Years' War (1618-1648)
        1.   Bohemian Phase
        2.   Danish Phase
        3.   Swedish Phase
        4.   Franco-Swedish Phase
    C.   Military Revolution?
    D.   Rebellions

II. Practice of Absolutism: Western Europe
    A.   France and Absolute Monarchy
        1.   Cardinal Richelieu's Centralization of Power under Louis XIII
        2.   Cardinal Mazarin during the Minority of Louis XIV
        3.   Reign of Louis XIV (1643-1715)
            a.   "The Sun King"
            b.   Control of State and Church
            c.   Finances and the Court at Versailles
            d.   Louis' Wars
    B.   Decline of Spain
        1.   Financial Troubles
        2.   Reforms by Guzman
        3.   Military Loses

III. Absolutism in Central, Eastern, and Northern Europe
    A.   German States
        1.   Brandenburg-Prussia
            a.   House of Hohenzollern
            b.   Frederick William's Army and his Commissariat
            c.   Elector Frederick III Becomes King Frederick I
        2.   Emergence of Austria
            a.   House of Habsburg
            b.   Leopold I's Move to the East
            c.   Multiculture Empire
    B.   Italy: From Spanish to Austrian Rule
    C.   Russia: from Fledgling Principality to Major Power
        1.   Reign of Ivan IV, the Terrible

       2. Reign of Peter I, (the Great) Romanov (1689-1725)
          a. Centralization of Authority
          b. Westernization
          c. Peter's Wars
   D. Great Northern States: Denmark and Sweden
   E. Ottoman Empire: Suleiman I
   F. Limits of Absolutism

IV. Limited Monarchies and Republics
   A. Weakness of the Polish Monarchy
       1. Elective System
       2. Confederation of Estates
   B. Golden Age of the Dutch Republic
       1. Independence following the Peace of Westphalia
       2. Economic Prosperity
       3. Amsterdam as a Commercial Capital
   C. England and the Emergence of Constitutional Monarchy
       1. James I and Parliament
       2. Charles I and Civil War
       3. Oliver Cromwell and the Commonwealth
       4. The Stuart Restoration and Charles II
       5. James II and the "Glorious Revolution"
       6. William and Mary and the Bill of Rights
       7. Responses to the English Revolution
          a. Thomas Hobbes and *Leviathan*
          b. John Locke and the Right of Revolution

V. World of Seventeenth-Century Culture
   A. Changes Faces of Art
       1. Mannerism: El Greco
       2. Baroque: Bernini and Gentileschi
       3. French Classicism: Poussin
       4. Dutch Realism: Leyster and Rembrandt
   B. Wondrous Age of Theater
       1. Shakespeare
       2. Lope de Vega
       3. Racine
       4. Molière

Chapter Summary

The political and religious crises of the sixteenth and early seventeenth centuries, with fears, wars, and rebellions, led philosophers and rulers to consider alternatives to what they considered the insecure and often chaotic institutional structures of the day. For over a century both groups defended the growth of strong monarchies that could keep the peace and order, who could enforce social uniformity, who could take measures to increase national prosperity.

Government moved increasingly toward absolutism, toward kings stronger than any known in Europe before, kings with power to provide order and prosperity. While absolutism reached its apex in France with the reign of Louis XIV, it had significant successes in Spain, the German states, Italy, Russia, and the Ottoman Empire. Everywhere there was a movement toward centralized power, the weakening of local rulers, and state control of economies.

Only in a few nations did royal power diminish and begin to share rule with parliamentary and constitutional systems. It did happen in Poland, in the United Provinces of Holland, and most importantly in Britain. In the latter there occurred in 1688 a bloodless revolution against James II, whom Parliament replaced with the dual monarchy of William and Mary, who promised certain rights to British citizens. There the way was paved not only for limited monarchy but also for democracy.

This Age of Absolutism was an age of cultural and philosophical achievement. El Greco's Mannerism and Bernini's Baroque styles were succeeded by the French Classicism of Poussin and the Dutch Realism of Rembrandt. It was an age when the French theater caught up with Shakespeare's English style and gained world dominance, as demonstrated by the work of Molière and Racine. It was a time of ferment in political theory: the penetrating analyses of Thomas Hobbes and John Locke. The Enlightenment was beginning.

Learning Objectives

1. Be able to analyze the causes and consequences of the witchcraft craze of the seventeenth century.

2. Describe the absolute monarchy of France, how it was established, how it functioned, and its effects on the nation.

3. Trace the rise of Russia to its status as a world power, giving particular attention to the life and work of Peter Romanov.

4. Examine the experience of the English monarchy in the seventeenth century, and show how it survived its rocky road.

5. Explain why the seventeenth century saw such a flowering of culture, particularly in art and literature, and discuss the achievements of its finest figures.

Glossary of Names and Terms

1. Peace of Westphalia: ended the Thirty Years' War by separating politics from religion and making the settlement along purely political lines.

2. Jacques Bossuet: advocate of the divine right of kings, by which their power was absolute and could not be disobeyed.

3. Cardinal Richelieu: chief minister to Louis XIII who established the administration under which the French kings could become absolute.

4. Edict of Fontainebleau: Louis XIV's attempt to make France Catholic by destroying Huguenot churches and schools, causing a mass emigration of skilled artisans.

5. Versailles: Louis XIV's grand palace, where he established his court and which he used to centralize the French government.

6. Gaspar de Guzman: his attempts to increase the power of the Spanish monarchy failed due to the number and strength of the aristocracy.

7. St. Petersburg: Peter Romanov's new capital city, built in the far north of Russia to rival the splendors of Versailles.

8. Glorious Revolution: the Protestant victory that exiled England's Catholic James I and brought William and Mary of Orange to the throne.

9. *Leviathan:* political work by Thomas Hobbes which defended absolute rule as the only way to provide a secure and proper life for citizens.

10. Rembrandt: greatest painter of the Dutch Golden Age who rejected material success to follow his own vision and died bankrupt.

Match the Following Words with their Definitions:

1. Mazarin

2. Fronde

3. Versailles

4. Oliver Cromwell

5. Bill of Rights

6. Thomas Hobbes

7. John Locke

8. El Greco

9. Nicholas Poussin

10. Jean-Baptist Racine

A. Argued that if a monarch broke his social contract, the people had the right to form a new government

B. Granted Parliament the right to levy taxes

C. Leader of the British Commonwealth

D. Mannerist master

E. Argued that order demanded absolute monarchy

F. Made use of themes taken from Greek tragedy

G. Center of Louis XIV's royal government

H. Rebellion of the French nobility against the royal family

I. Exemplified the principles of French Classicism

J. Directed the French government when Louis XIV was a child

Choose the Correct Answer:

1. One result of seventeenth century crises in Europe was

    a. an increased role of the church in secular society.
    b. a trend toward democratic reforms in government.
    c. the division of empires into smaller feudal kingdoms.
    d. a trend toward absolutism, as exemplified by Louis XIV.
    e. the rise in the number of slaves working there.

2. As Louis XIII's chief minister, Cardinal Richelieu was most successful in

    a. evicting the Huguenots from France.
    b. strengthening the central role of the monarchy.
    c. creating a reservoir of funds for the treasury.
    d. emerging victorious in the Fronde revolts.
    e. recruiting missionaries to go to China.

3. The series of noble revolts known as the Fronde resulted in

    a. the assassination in 1661 of Cardinal Mazarin.
    b. increased power for the Parlement of Paris.
    c. a stronger, more secure, more unified royal army.
    d. many Frenchmen looking to the crown for stability.
    e. the early coronation of Louis XIII's heir.

4. Louis XIV was most successful in controlling the administration of his kingdom by

    a. working closely with hereditary, aristocratic officeholders.
    b. using his intendants as direct royal agents.
    c. employing royal patronage to "bribe" officers to execute the king's policies.
    d. eliminating town councils and legislative bodies in the provinces.
    e. putting military officers in charge of judicial hearings.

5. Louis XIV restructured the policy-making machinery of the French government by

    a. personally dominating the actions of his ministers and secretaries.
    b. stacking the royal council with high nobles and royal princes.
    c. selecting his ministers from established aristocratic families.
    d. personally hearing every judicial case that was appealed from lower courts.
    e. advancing personally through every office, learning all their skills.

6. Louis XIV's military adventures resulted in

    a. French domination of Western Europe.
    b. defeat after defeat by coalitions of nations.
    c. the union of the thrones of France and Spain.
    d. increased popular support for Louis in France.
    e. the final victory of the French over the British worldwide.

7. Activities at the court of Versailles included all of the following *except*

    a. evenings of concerts, games, and banquets.
    b. attempts by aristocrats to catch the ear of the monarch.
    c. invitations to challenge Louis' authority.
    d. a system of etiquette that depended on the whim of the monarch.
    e. activities designed to demean noble visitors.

8. The overall practical purpose of the Palace of Versailles was to

    a. control and limit the power of the aristocracy.
    b. keep Louis' queen and mistresses happy.
    c. act as a reception hall for foreign visitors.
    d. give Louis a life of absolute privacy.
    e. allow Louis to recover from respiratory problems.

9. During the seventeenth century Spain

   a. grew rich off the spoils of its American colonies.
   b. lost most of her European possessions outside Iberia.
   c. curtailed the power of the Catholic Church.
   d. saw the emergence of a dominant middle class.
   e. benefited from the work of competent kings and first ministers.

10. The Russian "Time of Troubles" describes a

    a. period of anarchy before the rise of the Romanov dynasty.
    b. time of religious turmoil in which many Old Believers committed suicide.
    c. period of revolt led by Cossack Stenka Razin.
    d. part of the reign of Alexander I, when he reestablished serfdom in Russia.
    e. time of continual foreign invasion and famine.

11. The cultural reforms of Peter the Great

    a. failed to change habits of dress and grooming.
    b. left the Orthodox Church untouched.
    c. required Russian men to wear beards.
    d. permitted Russian women many new freedoms.
    e. required the use of French in all public schools.

12. In his efforts to Europeanize Russia, Peter

    a. required that Orthodox priests marry.
    b. reorganized the government so that the Duma shared power with him.
    c. adopted mercantilist policies to stimulate growth of the economy.
    d. built a "police state" with the aid of aristocratic bureaucrats.
    e. lowered taxes to stimulate free enterprise among the peasants.

13. Peter's primary foreign policy goal was to

    a. open a Russian warm-water port accessible to Europe.
    b. bring an end to the Ottoman Empire.
    c. defeat and control the Scandinavian countries.
    d. make Germany a Russian dependency.
    e. win a seat on the European Council of Elders.

14. The most successful absolute rulers of the seventeenth century were those who

    a. used traditional systems of administration to their advantage.
    b. completely crushed the power of the landed aristocracy.
    c. dominated the lives of their subjects at every level.
    d. established strict rules of dress and public behavior.
    e. held public executions as examples of the results of rebellion.

15. Between 1688 and 1832, Britain's government was in fact, if not in name

    a.   a plutocracy—ruled by the rich.
    b.   an oligarchy—ruled by an elite.
    c.   a theocracy—ruled by religious leaders.
    d.   an absolute monarchy—ruled by an all-powerful sovereign.
    e.   a democracy—ruled by the people.

16. The British Declaration of Rights and Bill of Rights

    a.   laid the foundation for a constitutional monarchy.
    b.   resolved England's seventeenth-century religious feuds.
    c.   reaffirmed the divine-right theory of kingship.
    d.   gave the king the right to raise armies without consent of Parliament.
    e.   ended the monarchy for the eleven years of the Protectorate.

17. The "Leviathan" of which Thomas Hobbes wrote was a

    a.   snake that killed a little Dutch boy.
    b.   mythical Frankish king who could serve as a role model for James II.
    c.   state with power enough to keep order.
    d.   ancient political principle of the right to revolution.
    e.   new invention that would make British ships more dependable.

18. All of the following are true of seventeenth century culture *except*

    a.   Bernini completed Saint Peter's Basilica.
    b.   Rembrandt left an immense fortune to medical science.
    c.   Lope de Vega wrote plays that he knew would please the public.
    d.   Racine used classical themes for his contemporary plays.
    e.   Molière satirized the religious and social practices of France.

19. One of the best examples of Baroque art is

    a.   El Greco's Toledo Altarpiece.
    b.   Rembrandt's Scenes of Amsterdam.
    c.   Poussin's Classical Dreamworld.
    d.   Bernini's Interior of Saint Peter's Basilica.
    e.   Judith Leyster's Scenes from Peasant Life.

20. Molière avoided legal harassment due to the

    a.   wealth and influence of his father.
    b.   immense popularity of his plays.
    c.   protection of Louis XIV.
    d.   intervention of the Archbishop of Paris.
    e.   use of Latin for phrases that might appear pornographic.

Complete the Following Sentences:

1. Henry IV had granted French Huguenots civil rights with his Edict of _____, but Louis XIV took them away with his Edict of _____.

2. Jean Baptiste Colbert, controller-general of _____ for Louis XIV, followed the policy of _____, encouraging _____, discouraging _____.

3. The suspicion that France and Spain would be united when Louis XIV's _____ became the Spanish King Philip V, led to the War of the _____ _____.

4. The Hohenzollern ruler who built the Prussian state, the Great Elector _____ _____, based his structure on a large and efficient _____ _____ and used a _____ to raise revenues.

5. In Italy, the three arms of the Counter-Reformation, the _____ , the _____, and the _____, long stifled all resistance to Catholic orthodoxy.

6. Peter Romanov decided after a trip to _____ Europe that Russia was a _____ _____ and needed an infusion of modern _____.

7. When it became evident to the English in 1688 that the baby son of King James II would perpetuate a _____ dynasty, they sent him into exile and chose as their monarchs William of _____ and his wife _____, the daughter of James II.

8. American and French used Englishman's John Locke's theories to demand _____ government, the rule of _____, and protection of _____.

9. The Golden Age of Dutch painting was financed by Dutch _____ and reached its zenith with the work of _____, who ironically in his later years eschewed _____ success.

10. In his play _____ Molière poked fun at the Paris _____, and in reaction they had it banned from the stage for _____ years.

Place the Following in Chronological Order and Give Dates:

1. Peter Romanov's trip to the West   1.

2. War of the Spanish Succession   2.

3. Turkish siege of Vienna   3.

4. England's Glorious Revolution   4.

5. Publication of Hobbes' *Leviathan*   5.

6. Michael Romanov begins his reign   6.

7. Edict of Fontainebleau   7.

Questions for Critical Thought

1. Outline the theory of Absolutism as propounded by Bodin and Bossuet; then and illustrate how it worked, using Louis XIV's France as your example.

2. Describe in detail the life of the aristocracy at Louis XIV's court in Versailles. To what extent was Louis master and to what extent a slave of his court?

3. What factors transformed the small German province of Brandenburg-Prussia into the core of what was to be a German nation? Explain each factor.

4. Describe Peter Romanov's role in the emergence of modern Russia. Was he more or less important for Russia than Louis XIV was for France? Explain your answer.

5. Name the European nations that became either limited monarchies or republics rather than absolute monarchies. In each case explain why it developed as it did—and did not.

6. Explain what made the Dutch so commercially successful in the seventeenth century. Why did so few other nations find such success? Give examples.

7. Describe the way a nearly-absolute monarchy became the world's first constitutional monarchy in Britain. What persons and events contributed to this change, and what part did each play?

8. List and explain the various political theories that grew out of the Age of Absolutism. Show how each one was a product of its specific time and place.

Analysis of Primary Source Documents

1. Explain how and why Suzanne Gaudry was condemned to death. What does her trial and its verdict say about French law and society in her day?

2. Describe the treatment of peasants on the farm captured by foreign soldiers during the Thirty Years' War, as recounted in the novel *Simplicius Simplicissimus*. To what extent do you see exaggeration for effect, and to what extent does this account agree with what you have read of treatment of civilians in other wars?

3. To what extent do Louis XIV's *Memoirs* show that he had thought the duties of a king? How well did his advice fit his own actions?

4. From Saint-Simon's account of Louis XIV's life, what do you conclude about the king's attitude toward women?

5. Explain how Peter Romanov's treatment of the rebellious Streltsy could be used to demonstrate Machiavelli's notion that the effective ruler must act without consideration for the usual principles of morality.

6. Explain how the 1688 British Bill of Rights paved the way for constitutional government. Show how this Bill influenced American colonists in the next century.

7. How much of Shakespeare's tribute to England in "Richard II" is patriotism, how much xenophobia, and how much the dramatist's wish to please his audience? Give examples of your opinion.

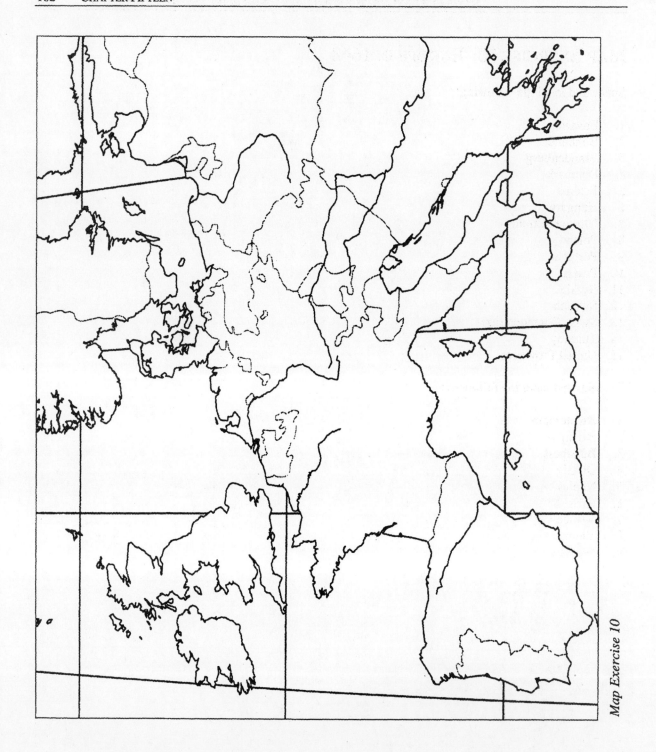

Map Exercise 10

MAP EXERCISE 10: EUROPE IN 1648

Shade and label the following:

1. Bavaria
2. Bohemia
3. Brandenburg
4. Denmark
5. Estonia
6. Hungary
7. Ottoman Empire
8. Poland
9. Portugal
10. Prussia
11. Russia
12. Sweden
13. Swiss Confederation
14. Tuscany
15. United Provinces

Pinpoint and label the following:

1. Amsterdam
2. Berlin
3. Budapest
4. Danzig
5. Naples
6. Paris
7. Venice
8. Vienna
9. Warsaw

CHAPTER SIXTEEN
TOWARD A NEW HEAVEN AND A NEW EARTH: THE SCIENTIFIC REVOLUTION AND THE EMERGENCE OF MODERN SCIENCE

Chapter Outline

I.   Background to the Scientific Revolution
     A.   Medieval Reliance on Classical Authority
     B.   Renaissance Scholars and the Discovery of Classical Disagreements
     C.   Artists and Close Observation of Nature
     D.   Early Modern Technological Innovations
     E.   New Mathematics
     F.   Hermetic Magic

II. Toward a New heaven: A Revolution in Astronomy
     A.   Ptolemy's Model: A Geocentric Universe
     B.   Copernicus
          1.   *On the Revolutions of the Heavenly Spheres*
          2.   Heliocentric Model
          3.   Church Reaction to Copernicus
     C.   Tycho Brahe and Johannes Kepler
          1.   Observations
          2.   "Music of the Spheres"
          3.   Planetary Laws
     D.   Galileo and Controversy
          1.   Galileo's Telescope
          2.   *The Starry Messenger*
          3.   Inquisition
          4.   Laws of Motion
     E.   Isaac Newton and Universal Physics
          1.   *Principia*
          2.   Universal Law of Gravity

III. Advances in Medicine
     A.   Influence of Galen
          1.   Animal Dissection
          2.   "Four Humors"
     B.   Paracelsus
          1.   Medicine as Chemistry
          2.   "Like Cures Like"
     C.   Andreas Vesalius
          1.   Human Dissection
          2.   Correction of Galen
     D.   William Harvey and the Human Blood System

IV. Women in the Origins of Modern Science
    A. Exclusion from Universities
    B. Margaret Cavendish: Inspiration to Women
    C. Maria Merian and Entomology
    D. Maria Winkelmann
        1. Discovery of a Comet
        2. Rejection by the Berlin Academy
    E. *Querelles des Femmes*
        1. Male Agreement about Female Inferiority
        2. Diminished Medical Role for Women

V. Toward a New Earth: Descartes, Rationalism, and a New View of Humankind
    A. Descartes' *Discourse on Method*
        1. Rejection of the Senses
        2. Separation of Mind and Matter
    B. Implications of Cartesian Dualism

VI. Scientific Method
    A. Francis Bacon
        1. *Great Instauration*
        2. Inductive Method
        3. Practical Uses of Science
    B. Rene Descartes' Emphasis on Deduction and Mathematics
    C. Isaac Newton's Synthesis of Bacon and Descartes

VII. Science and Religion in the Seventeenth Century
    A. Example of Galileo
        1. Split Between Science and Religion
        2. Attempts at a New Synthesis
    B. Benedict de Spinoza
        1. Panentheism
        2. Philosophy of Reason
    C. Blaise Pascal
        1. *Pensées*: Apology for the Christian Faith
        2. Limits of Science and Reason

VIII. Spread of Scientific Knowledge
    A. Scientific Societies
        1. Royal Society of England
        2. Royal Academy of France
        3. Scientific Journals
    B. Science and Society
        1. Acceptance through Practicality
        2. Science as a Means of Economic Progress and Social Stability

Chapter Summary

At the same time that kings were consolidating power and seeking a new social order based on absolute rule, an intellectual revolution took place which changed learned people's views of the universe, man's nature, and even the nature of truth itself. This revolution in science provided new models for heaven and for earth.

The Scientific Revolution began in the field of astronomy, and conclusions drawn by mathematicians and observers like Copernicus, Kepler, Galileo, and Newton both provided new understandings of the universe and its laws and called into question the wisdom of ancient and medieval scholars. Inspired by this study of astronomy and the realization that by empirical observation one can learn new things about the universe, scholars questioned and revised their opinions about medicine and the human sciences.

With the revolution in empirical studies came a new emphasis on human reason. Started by Rene Descartes and his famous *Discourse on Method*, the claims for rationalism focused attention on the nature and capacities of man's mind. While empiricism and rationalism were at times in conflict, they eventually merged to create a scholarship that rejected both tradition and authority in favor of continual reevaluation of established knowledge.

Religious doctrines were challenged and religious sensitivities ruffled by these secular endeavors, and scientists often found themselves at odds with religious powers. Even some of the scientists themselves were disturbed by the results of their studies. Pascal sought to reconcile science and religion, but his life was too brief to develop his ideas fully.

Yet science was too careful about its conclusions to be discredited and too useful to the world to be silenced. Scientific societies, sponsored by kings who saw benefits to their ambitions in science's achievements, disseminated amazing new discoveries and the general public enjoyed the fruits of scientific research. The modern world of progress and doubt was on its way.

Learning Objectives

1. Be able to trace the development of the science of astronomy from the work of Copernicus through that of Kepler, Galileo, and Newton.

2. Trace the development of the science of medicine from its early, primitive day through the discoveries of Paracelsus, Vesalius, and Harvey.

3. Explain the role that women played in the early years of modern science, recalling the obstacles that faced them.

4. Describe the competition between science and religion in the seventeenth century, and account for their inability to find common ground as Pascal longed to see.

5. Discuss the new scientific method of learning, the role of the scientific societies on its growth and influence, and the impact it had on European society.

Glossary of Names and Terms

1. Hermeticism: a belief that the world is a living embodiment of the divine and a magic-mathematical study the physical world can lead to God.

2. "Music of the Spheres": an early modern concept that creation, as demonstrated through its laws, has a harmony.

3. *Principia*: The work of Newton that captured and systematized all the laws of mechanics known to his day.

4. Paracelsus: early medical pioneer who believed that "like cures like" and gave drugs, often toxins, to his patients and kept records of his experiments.

5.   Vesalius: medical pioneer who publicly dissected cadavers and published his findings in his book *On the Fabric of the Human Body*.

6.   Margaret Cavendish: an aristocratic British woman scientist who, despite her recognized achievements, was excluded from the Royal Society on the basis of her gender.

7.   *Querelles des femmes*: literally "arguments about women," from the debates held by male scientists over whether women should be accepted as academic and professional equals.

8.   Francis Bacon: called for a total reconstruction of human knowledge, based now on scientific principles, which he gave concrete form.

9.   Pascal: French mathematician who began but did not live to complete a work called *Pensées*, which he hoped would bridge the gap he saw growing between science and religion.

10. *Journal des Savants*: magazine of new scientific discoveries issued by the French Royal Academy of Sciences, which helped members keep up with each other's work.

Match the Following Words with their Definitions:

1.   Nicholas Copernicus

2.   Tycho Brahe

3.   Johannes Kepler

4.   *The Starry Messenger*

5.   Isaac Newton

6.   William Harvey

7.   Maria Winkelmann

8.   Rene Descartes

9.   *Pensées*

10. Royal Academy of Sciences

A.   Advocated a geometric universe and tried to discover the "music of the spheres"

B.   Discovered the circulation of blood and showed it was caused by the pumping of the heart

C.   Astronomer denied a post in the Berlin Academy

D.   Made astronomical observations from an island given him by the King of Denmark

E.   Attempted to reconcile science and religion

F.   Louis IV's contribution to the French scientific revolution

G.   President of the Royal Society and only scientist buried in Westminster Abbey

H.   Regarded Ptolemy's geocentric universe as too complicated

I.   Advocate of rationalism who began his method with doubt

J.   Defended Copernicus' system

Choose the Correct Answer:

1.   The Scientific Revolution of the seventeenth century was

    a.   stimulated by a new interest in Galen and Aristotle.
    b.   a direct result of the revolt against social conditions in the Middle Ages
    c.   born in the Augustinian monasteries.
    d.   more a gradual building on the accomplishments of previous centuries than a sudden shift in thought.
    e.   the cause of consternation among the kings of Europe.

2.   The greatest achievements in science during the sixteenth and seventeenth centuries came in the areas of

    a.   astronomy, mechanics, and medicine.
    b.   astronomy, biology, and chemistry.
    c.   biology, mechanics, and ballistics.
    d.   engineering, physics, and dentistry.
    e.   anatomy, engineering, and medicine.

3.   The general conception of the universe prior to Copernicus held that

    a.   heaven was at the center and all creation circled it.
    b.   the earth was at a stationary center, orbited by perfect crystalline spheres.
    c.   the earth rested on the shell of a giant turtle.
    d.   it was all a mystery known only to theologians.
    e.   to ask questions about it might threaten the Christian faith.

4.   Although he made deductions about the construction of the universe, Copernicus was by formal training a

    a.   mathematician, specializing in Calculus.
    b.   banker attached to the Medici of Florence.
    c.   cloistered Augustinian monk.
    d.   military adviser to his uncle, an archbishop.
    e.   canon (church) lawyer.

5.   The universal theories proposed by Copernicus

    a.   led to his arrest and imprisonment in a monastery.
    b.   were supported by Protestants in order to make Catholics look provincial.
    c.   made the universe less complicated by discarding Ptolemy's epicycle theory.
    d.   explained the appearance of the sun's rotation with a theory of earthly rotation.
    e.   were later completely discredited by Newton.

6. Johannes Kepler believed that the truth of the universe could be found by combining the study of mathematics with that of

    a. Neoplatonic magic.
    b. Greek literary symbolism.
    c. the Book of Revelation.
    d. the Book of Daniel.
    e. papal dispensations.

7. Galileo held that the planets were

    a. composed of material much like that of earth.
    b. reflections of the divine city.
    c. spheres composed of pure energy.
    d. merely mirages in the "desert" of space.
    e. inhabited by creatures made by a rival to God.

8. Isaac Newton's scientific discoveries

    a. were met with great hostility from the Church of England.
    b. formed the basis for universal physics until well into the twentieth century.
    c. completely divorced God from the universe and its laws.
    d. were the first to be printed in a language other than Latin.
    e. alienated him both from the Royal Society and the English monarchy.

9. Newton's universal law of gravity

    a. offered an explanation for all motion in the universe.
    b. had little practical application to the questions of universal motion.
    c. showed that humans could never understand why God made things the way they are.
    d. seemed to indicate that the universe began with a "big bang."
    e. was lifted almost word for word from Copernicus.

10. Paracelsus revolutionized the world of medicine in the sixteenth century by

    a. disproving Galen's theory of two blood systems.
    b. dissecting human rather than animal cadavers.
    c. treating diseases with his "like cures like" method.
    d. rejecting "Christian Chemistry" as taught in the universities of his day.
    e. injecting himself with germs to note their effects.

11. The role of women in the Scientific Revolution was best characterized by

    a. the way scientific communities welcomed women as members.
    b. Maria Merian's breakthroughs in astronomy.
    c. the manner in which Margaret Cavendish debated science with men.
    d. Maria Winkelmann's professorship in physics at the University of Berlin.
    e. Spinoza's arguments for the full equal treatment of women.

12.   The overall effect of the Scientific Revolution on the *querelles des femmes* was to

    a.   dispel old myths about female inferiority.
    b.   increase the role of husbands in child care and education.
    c.   justify the continuation of male dominance in the field.
    d.   demonstrate that there was no inherent skeletal differences between the sexes.
    e.   break down old walls and permit women their proper place in the field.

13.   Maria Merian introduced to the field of science the importance of

    a.   sterilizing surgical instruments.
    b.   viewing heavenly bodies through smoked lenses rather than with the naked eye.
    c.   reconciling scientific findings with theological principles.
    d.   not judging a person's work by his or her gender.
    e.   providing precise illustrations of her subjects.

14.   Francis Bacon was important to the Scientific Revolution because of his emphasis on

    a.   experimentation and inductive reasoning.
    b.   pure, theoretical reasoning.
    c.   deductive conclusions, which moved from general to particular principles.
    d.   the obligation of scientists to protect nature.
    e.   reconciling science with religion.

15.   Organized religion in the seventeenth century

    a.   conceded that only science can explain the universe.
    b.   rejected scientific discoveries that conflicted with Christian theology's view of the universe.
    c.   cooperated as an equal and willing partner to the study of science.
    d.   simply ignored science, calling it a new "toy for the minds of God's children."
    e.   tried to imprison every scientist who threatened the faith.

16.   During the seventeenth century, royal and princely patronage of science

    a.   declined as science turned more and more to medicine.
    b.   was strongest in Italy and Spain.
    c.   became an international phenomenon.
    d.   replaced church funding of scientific research.
    e.   put severe limits on the scope of scientific experimentation.

17.   The scientific societies established the first

    a.   fundraising events for medical research.
    b.   journals describing the discoveries of members.
    c.   codes of ethics for the treatment of animals.
    d.   codes of ethics for the treatment of humans.
    e.   endowed chairs of science in the universities.

18.   Spinoza said that man's failure to understand the true nature of God leads to

    a.   a false worship of nature.
    b.   a society in which men use nature for selfish purposes.
    c.   a decline in the powers of moral judgment.
    d.   sexual permissiveness.
    e.   slavish devotion, exemplified by monastic deprivation.

19.   Blaise Pascal believed that

    a.   man can know God through pure reason.
    b.   man is the summation of all things.
    c.   Christians should trust only what God has revealed in Scripture.
    d.   god can be known only by the heart, not the reason.
    e.   faith and reason would find resolution given enough time.

20.   Science became an integral part of Western culture in the eighteenth century because

    a.   people came to see it as the only way to find the truth.
    b.   its mechanistic theories were popular with kings.
    c.   radical groups like the Levellers, when they came to power, insisted on the adoption of scientific laws.
    d.   it offered a new means of making profit and maintaining social order.
    e.   there was no alternative to its good sense.

Complete the Following Sentences:

1.   Renaissance humanists demonstrated that not all ancient scholars had agreed with
_____, _____, and _____, even though these men were accepted without question by medieval science.

2.   Early modern scientists agreed with Leonardo da Vinci that since God eternally _____, nature is inherently _____; yet these same scientists looked for the secrets of the universe through _____ magic.

3.   Copernicus rejected Ptolemy's _____ universe and postulated a _____ one because he found Ptolemy's system too _____.

4.   Peering through his telescope, Galileo discovered _____ on the moon, Jupiter's four _____, and _____ spots.

5.   Galileo explained the three approaches people might take to the new astronomy in his *Dialogue*, where three characters, _____, _____, and _____ argued the theory of Copernicus.

6.   During eighteen months in his home village, Isaac Newton invented _____, developed theories about the composition of _____, and began formulating the universal law of _____.

7.   Vesalius disputed Galen's assertion that blood vessels originate in the _____ but did not doubt his claim that two different kinds of blood flow through the _____ and _____.

8.   Descartes argued that man's _____ cannot be doubted but that the reality of the _____ _____ can and should be, thus creating what came to be called Cartesian _____.

9.   Although he was expelled from his Amsterdam _____ for heresy, Spinoza was actually a _____, not the atheist his critics claimed, believing that all things are in _____.

10.   The Royal Society was chartered in 1662 by _____, while the Royal Academy of Sciences was recognized in 1666 by _____. Both emphasized the _____ value of scientific research.

Place the Following in the Order of their Publications and Give Dates

1.   Harvey's *On the Motion of the*   1.
      Heart and Blood

2.   Newton's *Principia*   2.

3.   Copernicus' *On the Revolutions of the*   3.
      Heavenly Spheres

4.   Bacon's *The Great Instauration*   4.

5.   Descartes' *Discourse on Method*   5.

6.   Pascal's *Pensées*   6.

7.   Galileo's *The Starry Messenger*   7.

Questions for Critical Thought

1.   Discuss the causes of the Scientific Revolution of the seventeenth century. Of these causes, which seems strangest to modern minds? Why?

2.   What did the discoveries in seventeenth century astronomy contribute to the Scientific Revolution? What did each of the major astronomers add to the field?

3.   What three men added knowledge to the field of medicine during the seventeenth century? Briefly describe each one's contribution to the field.

4.   Describe the contribution of women to the Scientific Revolution. Why did male scientists have such difficulties accepting them as equals?

5.   Discuss the ways in which scientific discoveries affected the seventeenth century's image of man. How did the new image differ from the old one?

6.   Describe the "scientific method" that developed in the seventeenth century, and show how it was used in one of the emerging branches of science.

7.   How did the Scientific Revolution affect religious thought? How did religious thought affect the Revolution?

8.   What role did monarchs play in the Scientific Revolution? What were their motivations, and to what extent were their expectations realized?

Analysis of Primary Source Documents

1.   Using the *Life* of Jerome Cardan as your example, demonstrate the close relationship, as late as the sixteenth century, between science and what scientists today call superstition.

2.   Show how Copernicus' heliocentric theory was at the same time so simple and so profound.

3.   Describe the "tone" of the famous correspondence between Kepler and Galileo. How can you explain the apparent absence of jealousy usually associated with famous men?

4.   What personality traits can you find in Galileo's account of his astronomical observations that would explain why he was a successful scientist?

5.   Show how Isaac Newton's four rules of reasoning are the end result of two centuries in which the "scientific method" was developed and refined.

6.   Speculate on why—amid the scientific progress of his century and despite evidence to the contrary—Spinoza was so unprepared to accept women as equals.

7.   To what degree do you find Descartes' method for finding truth a good guide? Point out any difficulties one might meet applying it to contemporary scientific problems.

8.   What was at the root of Pascal's doubts about man's ability to find scientific certainty? What problems for science in the future did he accurately predict?

CHAPTER SEVENTEEN
THE EIGHTEENTH CENTURY: AN AGE OF ENLIGHTENMENT

Chapter Outline

I. The Enlightenment
  A. "Dare to Know" and the Laws of Human Society
  B. Paths to the Enlightenment
    1. Popular Understanding and Acceptance of Science
    2. A New Skepticism of Religion and Tradition
    3. Impact of Travel Literature
    4. Isaac Newton's Laws of Physics
    5. John Locke's Theory of Knowledge
  C. Philosophes and Their Ideas
    1. Montesquieu's Critique of Society and Government
    2. Voltaire's Critique of Justice and Religion
    3. Diderot's *Encyclopedia* and a New Way of Thinking
  D. A New "Science of Man"
    1. David Hume and the Birth of the New Human Science
    2. Quesnay and Laws Governing the Economy
    3. Adam Smith and *The Wealth of Nations*
  E. Later Enlightenment
    1. Condorcet and the Nine Stages of History
    2. Jean-Jacques Rousseau and *The Social Contract*
  F. "Woman's Question" in the Enlightenment
    1. Mary Astell and Sexual Equality
    2. Mary Wollstonecraft and Feminism
  G. Social Environment of the Philosophes
    1. Salons
    2. Secret Societies

II. Culture and Society in the Age of Enlightenment
  A. Innovations in Art
    1. Rococo: Watteau and Neumann
    2. Neoclassic Art: David
  B. Development of Music
    1. Baroque: Bach and Handel
    2. Classical: Haydn and Mozart
  C. Development of the Novel: Richardson and Fielding
  D. Writing of History: Voltaire and Gibbon
  E. High Culture of the Eighteenth Century
    1. Increased Readership: Magazines and Newspapers
    2. Education and Universities
    3. Crime and Punishment: Cesare Beccaria
    4. World of Medicine

      F.   Popular Culture
          1.   Festivals, Carnival, and Fairs
          2.   Chapbooks
          3.   Primary Education for the Masses

III.   Religion and the Churches
      A.   Institutional Church
          1.   Church and State: Jesuit Example
          2.   Toleration and the Jews
      B.   Popular Religion
          1.   Catholic Piety: Saints, Pilgrimages, Relics
          2.   Protestant Pietism: Moravian Brothers and Wesleyans

Chapter Summary

Each age builds upon the foundations of its predecessor, and never was this true to a greater degree than the way the eighteenth century built upon the seventeenth. The revolution in science led directly to the Enlightenment and its revolution in social philosophy.

The popularization of science, the subsequent growth of a healthy skepticism about tradition, the writings of world travelers, and the legacy of thinkers like John Locke and Isaac Newton brought about an eighteenth century flowering of philosophy which is considered one of the high points of Western civilization. The philosophes Montesquieu, Voltaire, Diderot, and Rousseau left a body of writings unsurpassed in the history of social commentary.

It was also an age of innovation in the arts. Rococo painting and architecture, classical music, and the birth of the novel form in literature all added style and color to the age. In the social sciences various writers began critically commenting on education, crime and punishment, and the social and economic causes behind historical events. The stage was set for modern scholarship and social criticism.

Christianity, which the philosophes blamed for many human woes, found itself in a hostile environment, with the institutional church branded archaic and intellectuals leaving it for what they considered a more respectable deism. Yet among the common people the traditional faith continued to have strong appeal and tenacity. A new era of piety swept both Protestant and Catholic camps; and England particularly experienced a new phenomenon, the popular revival meetings of the Wesleys.

Just as the Enlightenment was the product of the Scientific Revolution, so the Enlightenment ushered in the age of political revolution that followed it. It was both the child and the parent of revolution.

Learning Objectives

1.   Be able to discuss the ideas and trends that formed the foundation for the Enlightenment.

2.   Outline the assumptions and contributions to historical and human development of the philosophes.

3.   Describe eighteenth century innovations in the visual arts, music, literature, and the writing of history.

4.   Trace the changing attitudes toward social development, particularly crime and punishment, during the Age of Enlightenment.

5.   Examine the attitude toward religion, both established churches and popular piety, of people great and small during the Enlightenment period.

Glossary of Names and Terms

1. Montesquieu: French aristocrat whose work *The Spirit of the Laws* claimed that the key to good government was the separation of powers.

2. Denis Diderot: philosophe whose great contribution to the Enlightenment was the twenty-eight-volume *Encyclopedia*.

3. *Emile*: book in which Jean-Jacques Rousseau explained his revolutionary theories on education.

4. Mary Astell: English writer who advocated better educational opportunities for women and equality of the sexes in marriage.

5. *Vierzehnheiligen*: southern German pilgrimage church of the "fourteen saints" which illustrates the ideals of the Rococo style in architecture.

6. Franz Joseph Haydn: one of the masters of "classical" music, he was a prolific composer of music both for the court and the public.

7. Henry Fielding: a pioneer of the novel, he wrote about people without scruples who survived by their wits, including the character Tom Jones.

8. Cesare Beccaria: Italian reformer who argued that punishment should be designed to deter crime, not just to punish criminals.

9. Toleration Patent: Austrian Emperor Joseph II's decree of 1781 which granted religious toleration to minority faiths as well as to the majority Catholic population.

10. Methodism: the Anglican movement led by John Wesley which eventually separated from the Church of England to become a new denomination.

Match These Words with Their Definitions:

1.	Jean Calas	A.	Composer of the Baroque *St. Matthew's Passion*
2.	Deism	B.	Leading character in Henry Fielding's novel
3.	*Emile*	C.	Early magazine published by Addison and Steele
4.	Balthasar Neumann	D.	Belief in God as Creator without reference to Christian dogma
5.	J. S. Bach		
6.	W. A. Mozart	E.	Protestant defended by Voltaire when falsely accused of murder
7.	Tom Jones	F.	Expelled from France in 1764
8.	*Spectator*	G.	Rococo architect who built the Würzburg Residenz
9.	Jesuit	H.	Form of Protestant mysticism that emphasized good works
10.	Pietism	I.	Rousseau's imaginary student in his book on education
		J.	Prodigy who wrote *The Marriage of Figaro*

Choose the Correct Answer:

1.   Bernard de Fontenelle, the man who popularized the new scientific learning, was for fifty years secretary of the

     a.   Royal Academy of Science.
     b.   National Library of France.
     c.   Royal Society of Surgeons.
     d.   Jesuit Order in France.
     e.   International Order of Merit.

2.   The Enlightenment of the eighteenth century was characterized by the philosophes'

     a.   naive optimism that they could change society.
     b.   rejection of traditional Christian dogma.
     c.   emphasis on mysticism rather than rationalism.
     d.   revival of medieval Scholasticism.
     e.   active involvement in political movements.

3.   The French philosophes

     a.   fashioned a grand, rational system of thought.
     b.   flourished due to governmental patronage.
     c.   called for the state to suppress ideas contrary to their own.
     d.   left their families behind to live in communes.
     e.   strongly affected the religious thought of the common people.

4.   In his *Spirit of the Laws*, Montesquieu argued for

     a.   a strong monarchy to counteract social chaos.
     b.   the supremacy of legislatures.
     c.   elevating judiciaries to final, absolute power.
     d.   the end to all political disagreement and conflict.
     e.   balance between various branches of government.

5.   The form of religion called Deism was based on a

     a.   Newtonian view of the world as a machine created by God.
     b.   personal faith in God, the loving father of Jesus.
     c.   fervid and uncompromising atheism.
     d.   strong patriotism in which the state replaced the church.
     e.   pietistic belief in the basic goodness of man.

6.   Voltaire was perhaps best known for his criticism of

     a.   the militarism of the German states.
     b.   the modern idea of separation of church and state.
     c.   religious and social intolerance.
     d.   Renaissance admiration for the Greeks and Romans.
     e.   King Louis XIV.

7. Diderot's opinions on sexuality included

    a. a defense of the rights of homosexuals.
    b. the importance of ritual and tradition in marriage.
    c. an advocacy of strict and complete monogamy.
    d. the renunciation of chastity for the unmarried.
    e. the need for laws to control all sexual practices.

8. Cesare Beccaria challenged contemporary thought and practices concerning the

    a. relations of Church and State.
    b. proper punishment of criminals.
    c. practice of free love.
    d. popular election of governmental officials.
    e. absolute authority of kings.

9. Identify the correct relationship between the social scientist and his work.

    a. Cesare Beccaria—held that capital punishment was the most effective deterrent
        to crime.
    b. Francois Quesnay—tried to discover the natural economic laws that govern human society.
    c. Adam Smith—argued that the state should control the economy for the achievement of
        maximum profits.
    d. David Hume—tried to discover and explain to a general audience the natural laws of human
        sexuality.
    e. John Locke—argued for governmental "checks and balances" to achieve the maximum
        democracy.

10. In his *Social Contract*, Rousseau expressed the belief that

    a. governments are inherently evil and should be eliminated.
    b. the will of the individual is all-important to the social welfare.
    c. a society achieves freedom by doing what is best for all.
    d. a child is a small adult with adult abilities and obligations.
    e. love is pure only when unencumbered by marriage.

11. The rule of the eighteenth century salon was that

    a. no man would be admitted without a female companion.
    b. intellectual conversations would naturally lead to sexual relations.
    c. no women would be admitted unless accompanied by a man.
    d. relations between men and women would be purely platonic.
    e. nothing discussed there could be repeated outside the room.

12. Rococo architecture was

    a. largely confined to France.
    b. best expressed in the sculpture of Baron d'Holbach.
    c. best expressed in the buildings of Balthasar Neumann.
    d. characterized by strict geometrical patterns.
    e. doomed to extinction because of its cost.

13.   European music of the eighteenth century was exemplified by the

    a.   operas of Amadeus Mozart, who shifted the locus of music from Italy to Austria.
    b.   fireworks music of G.F.W. Handel, a prince who composed as a hobby.
    c.   highly elitist, abstract oratorios of Franz-Joseph Haydn.
    d.   loosely woven, secular, pastoral odes of Johann Sebastian Bach.
    e.   use of peasant tunes as comedy relief in oratorios.

14.   The historical literature of the eighteenth century

    a.   exhibited a growing preoccupation with politics.
    b.   was more what we call social science than literature.
    c.   paid careful attention to the economic and social causes of historical events.
    d.   generally praised the Middle Ages as a golden era.
    e.   attacked most of the social practices of the day.

15.   During the eighteenth century the British were pioneers in

    a.   Rococo architectural innovation.
    b.   the novel as a vehicle for fiction.
    c.   Baroque musical extravaganzas.
    d.   prison reform that swept all of Europe a century later.
    e.   criticism of royal privilege and power.

16.   Most eighteenth-century European educational institutions were

    a.   centers of innovation and intellectual adventure.
    b.   no longer connected with churches.
    c.   elitist and geared to the needs of the upper class.
    d.   concerned primarily with vocational education.
    e.   rapidly declining in enrollment.

17.   A noticeable trend in eighteenth-century medicine was the

    a.   dramatic improvement of hospital sanitation.
    b.   disappearance of folk practices like bleeding.
    c.   renewal of the practice of using leeches for transplants.
    d.   eradication of traditional forms of faith healing.
    e.   lessening of the older distinction between surgeon and physician.

18.   Literacy rates in late eighteenth-century France were

    a.   almost equal for men and women.
    b.   unchanged by the rise of an urban artisan class.
    c.   generally higher than in the century before.
    d.   in decline from rates in the previous century.
    e.   unknown due to the absence of accurate studies.

19. Because of its growing influence, the Society of Jesus was in 1773

    a.   given a new charter in keeping with its higher status.
    b.   granted homeland security in perpetuity in the Papal States.
    c.   cut down to half its size in order to increase efficiency.
    d.   dissolved by order of the pope.
    e.   ordered to increase its mission role in Asia.

20. Most eighteenth-century Christians believed that the solution to the "Jewish problem" was

    a.   religious tolerance for all minorities.
    b.   conversion to the Christian faith.
    c.   exile to the Americas or Africa.
    d.   exportation to a Jewish homeland in the Holy Land.
    e.   extermination.

Complete the Following Sentences:

1.   Pierre Bayle's famous _____ attacked traditional _____ practices and even assumptions about Biblical _____ such as King _____.

2.   Using the format of two Persian men visiting Europe, Montesquieu criticized the two main French institutions, the _____ _____ and the _____. In his *Spirit of the Laws* he praised British government for its _____ and _____.

3.   Voltaire, whose religious faith is termed _____, fought for religious tolerance and justice in the case of Protestant _____ _____, who was executed for the _____ of his _____.

4.   Diderot's multivolume contribution to Enlightenment thought, the _____, was attacked by censors for establishing "a spirit of _____ and _____."

5.   Among the Physiocrats, Scotsman Adam Smith criticized the economic _____ of his day, while Frenchman Francois Quesnay said _____ was the greatest source of wealth.

6.   Jean-Jacque Rousseau's interests roamed from government in his book *The _____ _____* to education in _____; and he blamed _____ _____ for the inequality of human society.

7.   The grace of Rococo is illustrated by Watteau's lyrical portrayals of _____ life and by Neumann's Pilgrimage Church of the _____.

8.   Music lovers today still celebrate the genius of Handel's great oratorio, *The _____*, and Mozart's "black comedy," _____ _____.

9.   The writing of history during the Enlightenment was given stature by Voltaire's study of the age of _____ and Gibbon's study of the decline and fall of the _____ _____.

10.   Although the Jesuits gained great influence by directing the _____ of young aristocrats, their image as an international network that threatened governments led to their expulsion from _____, _____, and _____.

Place the Following in Chronological Order and Give Dates:

1.   Publication of Adam Smith's *Wealth of Nations*   1.

2.   Publication of Rousseau's *Social Contract*   2.

3.   Publication of Montesquieu's *Persian Letters*   3.

4.   Publication of Condorcet's *Progress of the*   4.
      Human Mind

5.   Gibbon's *Decline and Fall of the*   5.
      Roman Empire completed

6.   Diderot's *Encyclopedia* begun   6.

7.   Publication of Voltaire's *Philosophic Letters*   7.

Questions for Critical Thought

1.   Name the major Enlightenment philosophes, and summarize what each of them contributed to the movement.

2.   What was the "New Science of Man" that arose during the Enlightenment? What were its roots, and what did it add to man's self-awareness?

3.   Describe innovations in art, music, and literature during the Enlightenment. How did Enlightenment philosophy encourage and mold these innovations?

4.   What observations about women made by Mary Wollstonecraft in 1792 do you hear being stressed by feminists today, two centuries later?

5.   Through what media and in what forms did the ideas of the philosophes reach the better educated members of the general public?

6.   At the same time that the philosophes were working to change the world, what was going on among the masses? Describe "popular" culture during the Enlightenment.

7.   What happened to the various "state churches" of Europe under the attacks of the Enlightenment critics?

8.   Describe popular religion—as opposed to institutional religions—during the Eighteenth Century. Why were the masses relatively unresponsive or hostile to the philosophes' attacks on religion?

Analysis of Primary Source Documents

1.   Summarize Montesquieu's theory of the separation of government powers, and show how he affected the thinking of those who created the American republic to come.

2.   Explain how and why Voltaire's attack on Christian intolerance proved so effective. How might an orthodox Christian have defended his faith against such attacks?

3.   Demonstrate with Diderot's *Voyage* the way the philosophes considered their thinking both highly sophisticated and "naturally" simple.

4.   Briefly state the two arguments: a) that Rousseau's "general will" leads to democracy; b) that it leads to totalitarianism. What do you think?

5.   Show how Mary Wollstonecraft appealed both to men and to women in her call for the rights of women. What kinds of people (men and women) would have responded favorably and what kinds would have responded unfavorably to her arguments?

6.   What reasons does the historian Edward Gibbon give for his general optimism about the future of the human race? What evidence do you find in his writings that he considers Europe the center of civilization?

7.   Defend, as an eighteenth-century judge might have done, the punishment inflicted on criminals, as recorded by Restif de la Bertonne. Then critique it.

8.   Describe the church services conducted by John Wesley and his Methodists. Explain why Wesley's Church of England did not welcome this movement.

CHAPTER EIGHTEEN
THE EIGHTEENTH CENTURY: EUROPEAN STATES, INTERNATIONAL WARS, AND SOCIAL CHANGE

Chapter Outline

I.   European States
     A. Enlightened Absolutism (?)
         1. Concept of Natural Rights
         2. Call for Enlightened Rulers
     B. Atlantic Seaboard States
         1. France: the Long Rule of Louis XV
         2. Great Britain: King and Parliament
             a. Prime Ministers
             b. John Wilkes
         3. Decline of the Dutch Republic
     C. Absolutism in Central and Eastern Europe
         1. Prussia: Army and Bureaucracy
         2. Austrian Empire of the Habsburgs
         3. Russia under Catherine the Great
         4. Destruction of Poland
     D. Mediterranean World
     E. Scandinavian States
     F. Enlightened Absolutism Revisited
         1. Rarity and Brevity
         2. Barriers of Reality

II. Wars and Diplomacy
     A. War of the Austrian Succession (1740-1748)
         1. Vulnerability of Maria Theresa
         2. Weak Peace of Aix-la-Chapelle
     B. Seven Years' War (1756-1763)
         1. European Theater
         2. Clive in India and Wolfe in Quebec
         3. British Victory
     C. European Armies and Warfare
         1. Class Divisions of the Armies
         2. Dramatic Increases in Size of Armies
         3. Maneuvers over Confrontation

III. Economic Expansion and Social Change
     A. Growth of the European Population
         1. Falling Death Rate
         2. Improvements in Diet
         3. Lingering Outbreaks of Disease
     B. Family, Marriage, and Birthrate Patterns
         1. Nuclear Family
         2. Treatment of Children of the Rich

     3. Suffering of Poor Children
     4. Late Marriages
     5. Women, Children, and Family Income
  C. Agricultural Revolution (?)
     1. Increase in Land under Cultivation
     2. Greater Supply of Meat
     3. Scientific Experiments in Agriculture
  D. New Methods of Finance
  E. European Industry
     1. Textiles and Cottage Industries
     2. New Methods and New Machines

IV. Social Order of the Eighteenth Century
  A. Peasants
     1. Domination by Wealthy Landowners
     2. Village As Center of Culture
     3. Poor Diet
  B. Nobility
     1. Military Service
     2. Country House
     3. Grand Tour
  C. Inhabitants of Towns and Cities
     1. Urban Oligarchies
     2. Growing Middle Class
     3. Laborers
     4. Problem of Poverty

Chapter Summary

While Europe experienced the scientific and intellectual revolutions of the seventeenth and eighteenth Centuries, its various states moved from early modern absolutism to the verge of republican revolution. Across the continent the Old Regimes experienced a set of crises in what can now be seen as preparation for the convulsions that later ushered in the modern age.

It was a time of what has been called "enlightened absolutism," although how enlightened the rulers were depends on the nation being studied. In Britain and Holland kingship gave way to representative government, even if those being represented were primarily members of the upper classes, while in France and Eastern Europe various forms and degrees of absolutism continued. In Prussia, for example, the Hohenzollerns gave their people efficiency and military glory without granting them civil rights, while in Austria the Emperor Joseph II tried to make Philosophy his lawmaker—but in the end believed he had failed.

Warfare became ever more efficient and deadly during the eighteenth century; and wars defined the future even more than they had in the century before. Prussia earned the right to stand among the strong nation-states because of its performance in the War of the Austrian Succession. Britain won the war for overseas empire with its several victories over France in the Seven Years' War.

Meanwhile populations continued to grow, and most European nations prospered. Yet the gap between rich and poor grew ever more pronounced, and poverty virtually overwhelmed organizations and government agencies that tried to do something to remedy it. The stage was set for social revolution and the military strife.

Learning Objectives

1.   Be able to compare and contrast the development of royal power in France and England during the eighteenth century and how this development affected each nation's future.

2.   Explain the reasons for the War of the Austrian Succession and how it reflected international relations on the European continent in the eighteenth century.

3.   Discuss trends in marriage, birthrates, and family life across the continent during the eighteenth century.

4.   Examine the new developments in industry and trade during the century, and show how they prepared the way for the modern era.

5.   Compare and contrast the lives of peasants, the nobility, and town and city dwellers during the century.

Glossary of Names and Terms

1.   United Kingdom: the nation created by the union of England and Scotland in 1707 under the Stuart dynasty.

2.   Pocket borough: an area of England where the local landlord had the only vote and usually elected himself to Parliament because he had the borough "in his pocket."

3.   Robert Walpole: leader of the British Parliament who under the Hanoverian kings fashioned the modern office of prime minister.

4.   Junkers: members of the Prussian landed nobility, used by Frederick William to staff his General Directory, his efficient bureaucracy.

5.   Frederick the Great: one of the best educated and most cultured monarchs of the eighteenth century, a diligent ruler who made the Prussian government and military both efficient and honest.

6.   Joseph II: ruler of Austria who abolished serfdom, freed up the economy, and gave religious toleration to all, explaining that he had made philosophy his lawgiver.

7.   Emelyan Pugachev: leader of a mass revolt against the rule of Catherine the Great, leading her to repress the Russian peasantry even more than before the uprising.

8.   Cottage industry: the small enterprise of the early industrial revolution in which spinners and weavers produced work in their own cottages.

9.   Grand Tour: a tradition among the young British aristocrats of traveling across the continent of Europe in search of adventure, love, and art treasures before settling down to married life.

10.   Order of St. Vincent de Paul: a Catholic example of the attempt by many churches to help the poor, like most of the others overwhelmed by the rapid increase in poverty.

Match These Words with Their Definitions:

1. Marie Antoinette

2. Robert Walpole

3. John Wilkes

4. Junkers

5. Maria Theresa

6. Montcalm

7. Jethro Tull

8. Richard Arkwright

9. Andrea Palladio

10. Sisters of Charity

A. Austrian empress who led political and fiscal reforms

B. Agriculture experimenter who advocated keeping soil loose for air and moisture

C. Architect whose classical style influenced country homes of aristocrats

D. Austrian wife of French King Louis XVI

E. Loser of an empire on the Plains of Abraham

F. Catholic organization dedicated to helping the poor

G. Prussian ruling class who held most army offices

H. Inventor of the "water frame" powered spinning wheel

I. British Prime Minister George I and II permitted to run their governments

J. Journalist member of the British parliament whose quarrel with royalty led to reform

Choose the Correct Answer:

1. France during the eighteenth century

    a. prospered under the enlightened philosopher-king Louis XV.
    b. suffered severe economic depression throughout the century.
    c. was torn apart by civil wars.
    d. lost an empire and acquired a huge public debt.
    e. secured its North American holdings against the British.

2. Political developments in eighteenth-century Britain included

    a. Parliament taking over the last remaining powers of the monarchy.
    b. the abolition of pocket boroughs to make elections more fair.
    c. calls for reform after the corrupt administration of Pitt the Younger.
    d. increased calls for more autonomy for the American colonies.
    e. the increased power of the king's ministers to make public policy.

3. The British aristocracy of the eighteenth century

    a. was split into two clearly and sharply divided groups in the House of Commons.
    b. allowed the monarchy to maintain some power because of its own factional struggles.
    c. lost many seats in Parliament to the growing merchant class of politicians.
    d. won seats in both houses through an equitable system of popular election.
    e. gave up all claim to the House of Commons and concentrated on controlling the House of Lords.

4. In the eighteenth century, Prussia's

    a. bureaucracy grew at an uncontrollable rate.
    b. bureaucracy and military were dominated by Junkers.
    c. reluctance to get involved in European wars cost her land.
    d. peasants used the civil service to win advancement.
    e. rulers initiated sweeping social reforms.

5. Prussia's Frederick the Great succeeded in

    a. imposing his strict Protestantism on a Catholic populace.
    b. crushing the power of the Prussian nobility.
    c. carrying out reforms that pleased the philosophes.
    d. making Prussia's scattered lands more unified and secure.
    e. marrying his sons to the strongest Catholic royal families.

6. The War of the Austrian Succession was caused by the fact that in 1740 the heir to the Austrian throne was a

    a. Woman, Maria Theresa.
    b. child, Joseph II.
    c. Catholic, Catherine of Germany.
    d. Protestant, James Stuart.
    e. Russian, Michael Romanov.

7. The Austrian emperor Joseph II

    a. reversed the enlightened reforms of his mother Maria Theresa.
    b. rescinded most of the privileges the Hungarians had enjoyed.
    c. stripped the nobility of all its former powers.
    d. was discouraged by the discontent that greeted his reforms.
    e. abdicated his throne during a peasant uprising.

8. The reforms of Joseph II included all of the following *except*

    a. complete religious toleration.
    b. the abolition of serfdom.
    c. construction of internal trade barriers.
    d. establishment of the principle of equality of all before the law.
    e. making German the language of the government.

9. Russia's Catherine the Great

    a. followed successfully a policy of expansion against the Turks.
    b. instigated enlightened reforms for the peasantry after the Pugachev revolt.
    c. alienated the nobility with her extensive enlightened reforms.
    d. had two of her sons assassinated to prevent further plotting against her.
    e. made a series of lovers Grand Dukes.

10. The partition of Poland in the late eighteenth century

    a.   occurred after decades of warfare with and between its neighbors.
    b.   was prevented by the military intervention of Thaddeus Kosciuszko.
    c.   showed that a nation in those days needed a strong king to survive.
    d.   none of the above
    e.   all of the above

11. Enlightened absolutism in the eighteenth century

    a.   never completely overcame the political and social realities of the day.
    b.   was most successful in strengthening administrative systems in the nation-states.
    c.   was limited to policies that did not undermine the interests of the nobility.
    d.   all of the above
    e.   none of the above

12. During the European phase of the Seven Years' War

    a.   Prussia defeated a combined force of Austrian, Russian, and French troops.
    b.   Frederick the Great won a battle at Rossbach in Saxony.
    c.   the dream of an European balance of power finally came to an end.
    d.   Peter III won decisive victories over the Prussians.
    e.   Austria gained control of Silesia.

13. Warfare on the continent of Europe during the eighteenth century was characterized by

    a.   reliance on mercenary armies.
    b.   ideological fervor that led to bloody battles.
    c.   limited objectives and elaborate maneuvers.
    d.   massive direct confrontations and pitched battles.
    e.   diplomatic maneuvering that saved thousands of lives.

14. The "agricultural revolution" of the eighteenth century came

    a.   because of the open field system.
    b.   in spite of an absence of new kinds of crops.
    c.   through the work of large landholders with new agricultural techniques.
    d.   despite the resistance of conservative aristocrats like Jethro Tull.
    e.   at a time of great famine.

15. Which of the following statements applies to Europe's social order in the eighteenth century?

    a.   It differed from the Middle Ages in that wealth became the sole determinate of social standing.
    b.   The nobility was homogeneous and served the same social function in all European countries.
    c.   The progress of the peasants was still hindered by services and fees they had to pay to powerful lords.
    d.   Peasants and nobles grew closer socially in Eastern Europe, where serfdom was eradicated.
    e.   England led the way in abolishing class distinctions and became an example of democracy for the rest of the continent.

16. During the eighteenth century European society saw

    a. earlier marriages and less divorce.
    b. newly married couples gaining independence from parents.
    c. a decline in the importance of the woman in the family's economy.
    d. laws that successfully ended infanticide.
    e. a great increase in the number of illegitimate births.

17. Population growth in the eighteenth century was due in part to

    a. much better hygienic conditions in cities.
    b. earlier marriages and longer periods of reproduction.
    c. exiling diseased people to foreign colonies.
    d. the end of the bubonic plague.
    e. all of the above

18. The eighteenth century European nobility

    a. played a large role in administering the rising nation-states.
    b. lost its old dominance in military affairs.
    c. composed right at twenty percent of Europe's population.
    d. differed little in wealth and power from state to state.
    e. was the bulwark of Christian orthodoxy across the continent.

19. The English nobility's country houses

    a. were secondary in importance to London town houses.
    b. architecturally reflected individualistic trends.
    c. reflected a growing male dominance.
    d. replaced the Grand Tour as a setting for the education of young male nobles.
    e. were constructed by serf labor.

20. The problem of eighteenth century European poverty was

    a. most chronic in Britain, which had programs of public relief.
    b. dramatically curtailed by the work of private religious organizations.
    c. made worse by the common belief that the poor were criminals.
    d. solved in France by public works projects.
    e. rarely discussed and largely ignored by officials or the aristocracy.

Complete the Following Sentences:

1. Because many seats in the British Parliament were controlled by one man—seats from what were called _____ boroughs—the House of Commons was dominated by the _____ _____.

2. William Pitt the Younger served King _____ through the times of the _____ Revolution and wars of _____.

3. Frederick the Great of Prussia loved learning so much that he invited the writer
_____ to live in his court; and as an enlightened ruler he wanted to grant his subjects
freedom of _____ and the _____ and religious _____.

4. When Joseph II succeeded his mother _____ _____ as sole ruler of Austria, he
announced that _____ would be the lawmaker of his empire.

5. The peasants' revolt against Catherine the Great of Russia was led by the Cossack
_____ _____, who was finally caught and _____, after which Catherine
treated as treason any calls for _____ _____.

6. In 1772 Poland was partitioned and lost _____% of its land and _____% of its people.
_____ more such partitions followed within a quarter century.

7. Outside Europe the Seven Years' War was fought in _____ and in _____
_____, all to determine whether Britain or France would have the greater world-wide
_____.

8. Rousseau's theories about children may have influenced upper class women to abandon the use of
_____ _____ to feed their babies and to begin buying _____ and _____
designed for children.

9. Jethro Tull produced higher crop yields by using a _____ to keep soil _____ and a
_____ for planting seed.

10. The young English aristocrat on his Grand Tour is said to have stopped in Paris to learn how to act
_____, in Florence to learn about _____, and in Venice to meet _____.

Place the Following in Chronological Order and Give Dates:

1.	Joseph II begins sole rule in Austria	1.
2.	Seven Years' War	2.
3.	Hanoverian Succession in Britain	3.
4.	Louis XVI begins reign in France	4.
5.	First Partition of Poland	5.
6.	Frederick the Great begins reign in Prussia	6.
7.	William Pitt the Younger retires from office	7.

Questions for Critical Thought

1. Define the term "Enlightened Despotism." Give three examples of enlightened despots of the
eighteenth century, show why they were given the title, and indicate how enlightened each one was.

2. Describe the events and personalities that moved Britain during the eighteenth century from absolute
to limited monarchy. Why did the same process not take place in France?

3. List three Central and Eastern European monarchies of the eighteenth century, and explain why or why not each of them is counted a success.

4. Describe the causes and results of the Seven Years' War. Explain why and how it was decisive for the colonial ambitions of Britain and France.

5. Discuss the progress made in eighteenth-century agriculture. What were the good and bad sides of such progress for peasants?

6. Contrast the lives of nobles and peasants in the eighteenth century. What factors prevented major social upheavals until late in the period?

7. Describe the peculiar phenomenon known as The Grand Tour. What purpose did it serve, and what did it generally accomplish?

8. How did thinking people of the eighteenth century explain the poverty of their age, and what remedies did they suggest? How effective were their remedies?

Analysis of Primary Source Documents

1. Describe Louis XVI's nightly *coucher*. What purposes did such a ritual serve? What was the method behind his madness?

2. After reading the correspondence between Frederick of Prussia and his father, how would you think he probably described "the old man" to trusted friends his own age?

3. What does the description Catherine gave of her early life tell you about her self-image as a child? Why would she write so vividly of her early trials and the problems she had to overcome?

4. What does Clive's letter describing the Battle of Plassey say about the temperament needed to be a successful eighteenth-century British overseas general? What hints does it give as to the reason Britain won its wars for empire?

5. What does Sheridan's play tell you about the lives of British aristocrats of the eighteenth century? In what ways does wealth and position give them privilege, and in what ways are they still bound by medieval custom? What would you suggest Jack say to his father's arrangements?

6. What clues do you find in Arthur Young's *Travels* that he may have arranged his "findings" to prove the superiority of English agricultural practices?

7. How does the British Woolen Workers' Petition of 1786 reflect the two conflicting definitions of "progress" in that day?

8. Describe a debate that might have occurred between an advocate of free market economy and one who believes in government programs to help the poor in eighteenth-century France.

CHAPTER NINETEEN
A REVOLUTION IN POLITICS: THE ERA OF THE FRENCH REVOLUTION AND NAPOLEON

Chapter Outline

I.   Beginnings of the Revolutionary Age: The American Revolution
    A.   War for Independence
        1.   Taxes
        2.   Crises
        3.   Why the Colonies Won
    B.   Forming a New Nation
        1.   Constitution
        2.   Bill of Rights
    C.   Impact America's Revolution on Europe

II. Background to the French Revolution
    A.   Social Structure of the Old Regime
        1.   First and Second Estates
        2.   Third Estate
    B.   Other Problems Facing the French Monarchy
        1.   Privileges
        2.   Finances

III. French Revolution
    A.   From Estates-General to National Assembly
        1.   National Assembly
        2.   Common People Intervene
    B.   Destruction of the Old Regime
        1.   Declaration of the Rights of Man and the Citizen
        2.   Women's March
        3.   Catholic Church
        4.   New Constitution
        5.   Opposition from Within and Abroad
    C.   Radical Revolution
        1.   Proclamation of a Republic
        2.   Execution of Louis XVI
        3.   A Nation in Arms
        4.   Committee of Public Safety and the Reign of Terror
        5.   "Republic of Virtue"
        6.   Dechristianization and A New Calendar
        7.   Equality and Slavery
        8.   Decline and Fall of the Committee of Public Safety
    D.   Thermidorean Reaction and the Directory

III. Age of Napoleon
    A.   Rise to Power
        1.   Military Victory in Italy and Losses in Egypt

2. Consul (1799-1804)
3. Emperor (1804-1815)
B. Domestic Policies of Emperor Napoleon
   1. Concordat with the Church
   2. Code Napoleon
   3. Bureaucracy
   4. Growing Despotism
C. Napoleon's Empire and Europe's Response
   1. The Three Divisions: France, Dependent States, Allied States
   2. Obedience and Liberties
   3. Destruction of the Old Order
   4. Europe's Reaction and British Nationalism
   5. Russian Fiasco
   6. Elba, Waterloo, and St. Helena

Chapter Summary

The late eighteenth century saw the coming of a revolution that combined the ideals of the philosophes with the frustrations of social and economic groups long denied equal rights and powers in the nation-states. Europe and indeed the world were never the same again.

The revolution began, of all places, in the British colonies along the east coast of North America. Pushed to rebellion by a growing dissatisfaction with the way Britain administered their affairs, particularly the system of taxation, the colonists declared their independence and to the world's surprise, but not without the world's help, achieved it. They then established a republic based on the ideals of the European Enlightenment. The example was not lost on Europeans.

Within a decade of America's independence, when Louis XVI of France called his Estates-General to help him raise revenues, the Third Estate declared itself a national Assembly and proceeded to initiate the French Revolution. Through the rest of the century France reordered the Old Regime and incurred the wrath of the kings of Europe. When the radical phase of the revolution went too far and France found herself beset with enemies on every side, a conservative reaction set in and led to the rise of the "liberal" dictator who made himself emperor of the French, Napoleon Bonaparte.

For a decade Napoleon remade the map of Europe, using military genius to bring the liberal ideals of the revolution to the nations he conquered. Even after he was defeated and exiled, after royal figures were restored to their thrones, the spirit of the French Revolution lived on to inspire succeeding generations. The world in which we live was truly born in these revolutions of the late eighteenth and early nineteenth centuries.

Learning Objectives

1. Be able to discuss objectively the causes and consequences of the American War for Independence.

2. Explain why and how the French Old Regime was destroyed and the consequences for subsequent European history.

3. Examine the reasons why the French Revolution turned radical and violent and how this affected the career of Napoleon.

4. Trace the rise of Napoleon and how he restructured France as he redirected the energies of the revolution.

5. Recount the way Napoleon created his empire, why it did not last, and its effects on nations outside France.

Glossary of Names and Terms

1. Articles of Confederation: the first constitution of the new United States of America, later dropped for the Constitution of 1788.

2. Lafayette: French military officer who served with George Washington in the American War for Independence and returned home with republican ideals.

3. Ségur Law: an attempt to curtail the sale of military offices to members of the rising French middle class in order to prevent the nobility from growing.

4. Bourgeoisie: the French middle class, which in the eighteenth century was growing in economic worth but not in political power.

5. National Assembly: the name the Third Estate assumed after taking the Tennis Court Oath not to adjourn until it had given France a constitution.

6. Bastille: the "prison" in central Paris taken and "liberated" by a mob on July 14, 1789, signaling the beginning of the popular phase of the French Revolution.

7. Jacobins: the most radical party in the early days of the revolution, their name taken from the fact that they met in a former Jacobin convent.

8. Committee of Public Safety: the governing body of France during the radical phase of the revolution, the members precipitated the reign of terror.

9. Temple of Reason: the name given to the Cathedral of Notre-Dame in Paris, signifying that France had been dechristianized.

10. *Code Napoleon*: the Civil Code of the Emperor Napoleon, who granted to France and its empire many of the rights demanded by the French revolutionaries.

Match These Words with Their Definitions:

1.	Articles of Confederation	A.	Fought with Americans to "strike a blow against England"
2.	Lafayette	B.	Radical deputies in the French National Assembly
3.	Bastille	C.	Revolutionary name for Notre Dame Cathedral
4.	Jacobins	D.	Provincials who protected the life of Louis XVI
5.	Girondins	E.	Site of naval battle which led Napoleon to adopt the Continental System
6.	Temple of Reason		
7.	Toussaint	F.	The month in which the French Revolution took a conservative turn
8.	Thermidor	G.	First a symbol of oppression and later of freedom
9.	Concordat	H.	Leader of the Haitian Revolution
10.	Trafalgar	I.	Demonstrated Napoleon's pragmatic policy toward religion
		J.	Scrapped at Philadelphia in 1787

Choose the Correct Answer:

1.   After 1763 British authorities and American colonists came into conflict over

     a.   methods of raising revenue.
     b.   expansion west of the Mississippi River.
     c.   freedom of religious expression.
     d.   treatment of French prisoners of war.
     e.   treatment of Indian prisoners of war.

2.   Of paramount importance to the American victory over the British was

     a.   British weakness on the seas.
     b.   Spain's treachery in the western territories.
     c.   the military and financial assistance of France.
     d.   a lack of discipline in the British ranks.
     e.   the superior training of American officers.

3.   The United States Constitution of 1789 was

     a.   a revision of the Articles of Confederation.
     b.   viewed by European liberals as too utopian to last.
     c.   seen by Europeans as the fulfillment of Enlightenment dreams.
     d.   of little or no influence on the French Revolution.
     e.   passed by the states because of its Bill of Rights.

4.   By the eighteenth century the French nobility and bourgeoisie were

     a.   growing farther apart in social status.
     b.   increasingly less distinguishable from each other.
     c.   rapidly losing social status to the peasants.
     d.   frequently involved in street fights.
     e.   of different religious affiliations.

5.   The immediate cause of the French Revolution was

     a.   military and naval losses to Britain.
     b.   a series of financial reversals.
     c.   religious turmoil between Catholics and Huguenots.
     d.   a dispute over the ideas of Voltaire.
     e.   the lavish lifestyle of the monarchy.

6.   The controversy over voting by order rather than voting by head in the Estates-General led
     eventually to

     a.   a motion by the Nobles of the Robe to adjourn.
     b.   a move by "lovers of liberty" to stop all voting.
     c.   the expulsion of the Third Estate.
     d.   the withdrawal of the Third Estate to form a National Assembly.
     e.   direct intervention by Louis XVI.

7. The Declaration of the Rights of Man and Citizen

    a. was issued by Louis XVI to end the rebellion.
    b. was introduced to the Estates-General by a delegation of philosophes.
    c. owed much to the American Declaration of Independence.
    d. kept all aristocratic privileges intact.
    e. made it clear that the word "man" referred both to males and females.

8. The Jacobins took their name from

    a. one of the radical delegates to the Assembly, Jacques le Boulanger.
    b. the younger brother of Louis XVI.
    c. the Old Testament patriarch who led his Hebrew people out of Egyptian slavery.
    d. one of the more prominent philosophes, Jacobus Colet.
    e. the convent in Paris where they often met.

9. During the years 1792 and 1793, the city of Paris was

    a. controlled by a Commune that favored radical change.
    b. first to support the Constitution of the Year Four.
    c. where Napoleon first won a popular election.
    d. stripped of all religious names and symbols.
    e. often on fire after radical demonstrations.

10. Historians have noted that the French Revolutionary Army

    a. helped create the modern concept of nationalism.
    b. initiated the modern system of officer training and ranking.
    c. perfected the techniques and ethics of total war.
    d. began the radical practice of showing no mercy to prisoners.
    e. was used only to defend France when it was attacked.

11. In its attempt to "preserve" the revolution from its internal enemies, the Committee of Public Safety

    a. singled out the nobility for total annihilation.
    b. brutally crushed cities that rebelled against the government.
    c. used the guillotine only on members of the lower class.
    d. considered restoring the Bourbons to power.
    e. relied on the moral persuasion of the clergy.

12. During the revolution, French women

    a. generally worked quietly behind the scenes.
    b. received encouragement to speak out from French men.
    c. limited their demonstrations to protests against food shortages.
    d. were not allowed to participate in political activities.
    e. died in far greater numbers than men.

13. The republican calendar of 1793

    a.   named nine of the twelve months after philosophes.
    b.   contributed to the overall plan of dechristianization.
    c.   was well received by most of the people.
    d.   survived the Napoleonic Era.
    e.   influenced calendars in many other countries during the nineteenth century.

14. The program of dechristianization did *not* include

    a.   a new calendar without religious holidays.
    b.   removal of saints' names from street signs.
    c.   a systematic execution of bishops.
    d.   changing the names of church buildings.
    e.   encouraging priests to marry.

15. After the Thermidorean Reaction, the Directory government

    a.   relied primarily on the support of royalists.
    b.   was elected directly by universal franchise.
    c.   generally had wise and honest financial leadership.
    d.   saw to it that Napoleon was raised to leadership.
    e.   relied heavily on military support for its survival.

16. Which of the following statements best applies to Napoleon?

    a.   He was the child both of the Enlightenment and the Revolution.
    b.   He had a deep sense of moral responsibility to the people of France.
    c.   He advocated an invasion of Britain in the 1770s.
    d.   He was born the illegitimate son of a Corsican priest.
    e.   He had no formal military training before he volunteered for army service.

17. Which of the following statements best applies to Napoleon's domestic policies?

    a.   In order to promote democracy, he granted great autonomy to provincial administrations and
          their elected officials.
    b.   His "new aristocracy" was based on wealth and privilege as well as birth.
    c.   His Civil Code reaffirmed the ideals of the Revolution and established a uniform legal system.
    d.   In order to win church support, he reestablished Catholicism as the official state religion of
          France.
    e.   In order to promote stability, he made it virtually impossible to get a divorce.

18. Napoleon's Grand Empire

    a.   was composed of three parts but held together by loyalty to him.
    b.   revived the power of the nobility and clergy in all conquered territories.
    c.   included all of Europe after 1805.
    d.   left dependent states free to choose their own royal families.
    e.   had no long-term impact on the allied states.

19. Napoleon sought to bring Britain to its knees by

    a.   launching two unsuccessful invasions across the English Channel.
    b.   preventing Britain from trading with the continent.
    c.   fomenting and military supporting a Scottish war for independence.
    d.   giving arms to the rebellious Irish Republican Army.
    e.   bringing the United States into the European war.

20. Napoleon's decision to invade Russia stemmed from

    a.   his desire to bring liberal reforms to that country.
    b.   France's need for raw materials to continue its wars.
    c.   England's threat to invade the continent through Poland.
    d.   Russia's defection from his Continental System.
    e.   a letter intercepted by spies that indicated Russia planned to attack France.

Complete the Following Sentences:

1. At the time of the French Revolution both the nobility of the _____ and the nobility of the _____ sought to extend their powers at the expense of the _____.

2. At the time of the French Revolution the bourgeoisie included _____, _____, and _____, all of whom sought security and status through the purchase of _____.

3. Hoping that the Estates-General would help him get through a _____ crisis then gripping France, Louis XVI called it into session at _____ in May, 1789, unintentionally opening the way for the French _____.

4. Under the Civil Constitution of the Clergy, bishops and priests were to be elected by the _____ and paid by the _____, but a majority of the French _____ refused to support it.

5. In debates late in 1792 over the fate of Louis XVI, the _____ faction favored keeping him alive while the _____ called for his execution, and early in 1793 the _____ won.

6. The movement of dechristianization removed the prefix _____ from street signs, changed the name of the Cathedral of _____ _____, and pressured Catholic priests to _____.

7. In the revolutionary calendar, months were named for natural, agricultural events, such as _____ for mist, _____ for seeding, and _____ for ripening.

8. Robespierre's attempt to create a Republic of _____ led eventually to his own execution at the _____ and an end to the _____ phase of the revolution.

9. Napoleon attempted to strike indirectly at Britain in _____, which would block her route to India, but when he failed he _____ his army and returned to _____.

10. After his first exile on _____, Napoleon returned to rule France for three months, until his defeat at _____ and final exile on _____ _____.

Place the Following in Chronological Order and Give Dates:

1. American Bill of Rights   1.

2. Battle of Waterloo   2.

3. Continental System established   3.

4. Storming of the Bastille   4.

5. Declaration of American Independence   5.

6. Napoleon's coronation as emperor   6.

7. Execution of Louis XVI   7.

Questions for Critical Thought

1. Outline the system of government adopted by the American republic, and show why many Europeans considered it the fulfillment of Enlightenment dreams.

2. Describe French society and government just before the French Revolution. What characteristics were most responsible for the upheaval that began in 1789?

3. Outline the major events of the French Revolution from 1789 through 1804, and discuss four general principles of revolution to be found in this picture.

4. Why did the French Revolution turn radical? What forms did the radical phase take, and what were the final results?

5. What steps did the French revolutionaries take in 1783 through 1794 to ensure that there could be no return to the Old Regime? To what extent were they and were they not successful?

6. List and discuss the major events that brought Napoleon Bonaparte to power in France. At what points might he have been stopped? How?

7. Evaluate Napoleon as a military man and as a head of state. Did he fulfill or betray the revolution? Explain your conclusion.

8. Why did Napoleon fall? With your hindsight, how would you have advised him to avoid his demise? How successful do you feel you would have been advising him?

Analysis of Primary Source Documents

1. Pretend you are a moderate member of the British Parliament and have just read the American Declaration of Independence. What would you say in your next speech to that body?

2. Describe the storming of the Bastille, and explain why this bloody event came to symbolize the French "triumph of justice and liberty."

3. What parts of the "Declaration of the Rights of Man" were derived from the writings of the philosophes, and what parts went beyond them?

4. What specific claims made by the "Declaration of the Rights of Woman" prevent one from mistakenly assuming that it is a document from the 1990s rather than the 1790s?

5. Use the description of an execution during the Reign of Terror to demonstrate the moral level to which the French Revolution had reduced people. Speculate on whether this must always be so.

6. It has been said that the words of Robespierre defending violence in the name of liberty could be the words of Lenin defending it in the name of communism. Explain how this might be true.

7. Pick out the words (nouns, adjectives, verbs) Napoleon used to create images and emotions that would inspire courage and determination among his men.

8. Which side would Napoleon have taken in the debate among historians: Does the age make the man or the man the age? How would he have defended his position?

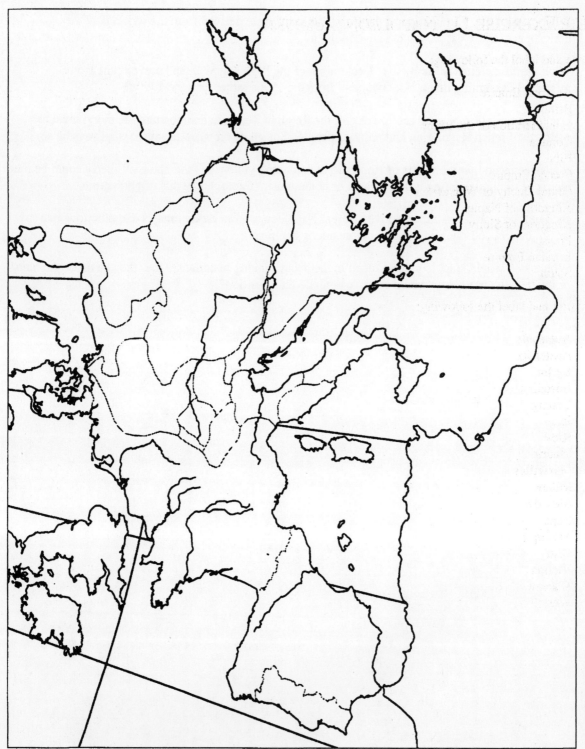

Map Exercise 11

MAP EXERCISE 11: NAPOLEON'S EMPIRE

Shade and label the following:

1. Austrian Empire
2. Britain
3. Confederation of the Rhine
4. Corsica
5. Elba
6. French Empire
7. Grand Duchy of Warsaw
8. Kingdom of Naples
9. Kingdom of Sicily
10. Prussia
11. Russian Empire
12. Spain

Pinpoint and label the following:

1. Auerstadt
2. Austerlitz
3. Berlin
4. Borodino
5. Danzig
6. Jena
7. Kiev
8. Madrid
9. Marseilles
10. Milan
11. Moscow
12. Paris
13. Trafalgar
14. Ulm
15. Vienna
16. Warsaw
17. Waterloo

CHAPTER TWENTY
THE INDUSTRIAL REVOLUTION AND ITS IMPACT ON EUROPEAN SOCIETY

Chapter Outline

I. Industrial Revolution in Great Britain
    A. Origins and Causes
        1. Capital for Investment
        2. Early entrepreneurs
        3. Mineral Resources
        4. Government Favorable to Business
        5. Supply of Markets
    B. Technological Changes and New Forms of Industrial Organization
        1. Cotton Industry's Power Looms
        2. James Watt's Steam Engine
        3. Iron Industry
        4. Revolution in Transportation
            a. Richard Trevithick's Locomotive
            b. George Stephenson's *Rocket*
        5. Industrial Factory
    C. Great Exhibition of 1851
        1. Leadership of Prince Albert
        2. Britain as Industrial Leader

II. Spread of Industrialism
    A. What Limited Its Spread
        1. Lack of Transportation Systems
        2. Traditional Habits of Business
        3. Upheaval of Wars
        4. Lack of Technical Education
    B. What Encouraged Its Spread
        1. Entrepreneurs with Technical and Business Skills
        2. Technical Schools
        3. Government Support
        4. Joint-Stock Investment Banks
    C. Centers of Continental Industrialization
        1. Belgium
        2. France
        3. Germany
    D. Industrial Revolution in the United States
        1. Building of a System of Transportation
        2. A Labor Supply from Rural New England
        3. The Capital-Intensive Pattern
    E. Limiting Industrialism in the Non-industrial World

III. Social Impact of the Industrial Revolution
    A. Population Growth and the Great Hunger
    B. Growth of Cities
        1. Irresponsible and Irresponsive Governments
        2. Wretched Sanitary Conditions
        3. Adulteration of Food
        4. Reforms of Edwin Chadwick
    C. New Industrial Middle Class
        1. Out of Mercantile Trades
        2. Out of Dissenting Religious Minorities
        3. To a New Elite
    D. New Working Class
        1. Laborers
        2. Servants
        3. Working Conditions
            a. In the Mines
            b. Pauper Apprentices
            c. Child Labor
            d. Women Workers
            e. Factory Acts At Last
    E. Standards of Living for Workers
        1. Wild Fluctuations of Wages and Prices
        2. Periodic Overproduction and Unemployment
    F. Worker Efforts at Change
        1. Robert Owen's Utopian Socialism
        2. Trade Unions
        3. Luddite Attacks on Machinery
        4. Chartism's Petition to Parliament
    G. Government Efforts at Change
        1. Factory Act of 1833
        2. Coal Mines Act of 1842

Chapter Summary

The Industrial Revolution that came first to Britain and then to the Continent of Europe changed the political and social order of Western people fully as much as the religious revolution called the Reformation, the intellectual revolution of the Enlightenment, or the political revolutions that followed the French Revolution. In many ways it changed the lives of the common worker more than the previous revolutions.

The Industrial Revolution started in Britain, where inventions, organizational skills, and natural resources combined to remake the countryside and the cities. It spread after a generation to the continent, particularly to places that had the same natural resources and organizational systems as Britain's, and by the middle of the nineteenth century had redefined society. The Great Exhibition of 1851 in London demonstrated the achievements but did not point out the human suffering that accompanied those achievements.

The social impact of the Industrial Revolution is still being observed and assessed. A tremendous growth in city populations, the creation of a new middle class and a working class, an ever increasing gap in earnings and quality of life between owners and workers all helped to make the modern age what it has been for a century—for better and for worse. The most striking losers in this new age were for many decades the children who were literally "used up" to supply labor for factories.

Eventually reaction came. The workers themselves, however limited their powers might be, began calling for more rights to determine their work and lives; and social reformers made the case of the workers so articulately that at last governments had to respond. The class struggle of modern times was underway.

Learning Objectives

1. Be able to explain why Britain was the first nation to be industrialized and how it was accomplished.

2. Trace the spread of the industrial revolution onto the continent of Europe and to the United States and show how it differed from country to country.

3. Explain how industrialization affected population growth and life in cities.

4. Describe the effect industrialization had on class structures and the new ways of life for each of the new classes.

5. Outline the various plans of reform offered by people concerned with the working and living conditions of urban laborers and what happened to each plan.

Glossary of Names and Terms

1. Capital: liquid assets (usually cash) which can readily be moved from place to place and invested in new forms of enterprise.

2. Edmund Cartwright: inventor of the power loom, which increased the production of cloth and precipitated the British industrial revolution.

3. *The Rocket*: the first locomotive used on the first public railway line, invented by George Stephenson and in full operation by the 1830s.

4. Great Exhibition: the first "world's fair," held in Kensington in 1851 to demonstrate the industrial might and superiority of Great Britain.

5. Darmstadt Bank: the main German version of the joint-stock corporation, which used the savings of small investors to open new businesses.

6. Great Famine: the human tragedy in Ireland when in 1845 the potato crop failed and over a million people starved.

7. Edwin Chadwick: secretary of the British Poor Law Commission who headed a study of living conditions in urban slums.

8. Robert Owen: factory owners and utopian reformer who created cooperative rather than competitive working communities.

9. Luddites: skilled craftsmen of the British midlands who physically attacked the machines they felt were taking away their jobs.

10. Chartism: the British movement that petitioned Parliament in the 1840s to grant universal male suffrage and the elimination of property qualifications for Parliamentary membership.

Match These Words with Their Definitions:

1. Edmund Cartwright

2. James Watt

3. George Stephenson

4. Crystal Palace

5. Friedrich List

6. *Crédit Mobilier*

7. *Kreditanstalt*

8. Ruhr Valley

9. Edwin Chadwick

10. Robert Owen

A. Site of the Great Exhibition of 1851

B. Site of Germany's rich coal resources

C. Lawyer who championed the cause of the urban poor

D. Inventor of the power weaving loom

E. Inventor of the steam engine

F. Advocate of rapid industrialization and the use of tariffs

G. Industrial joint stock corporation of Vienna

H. His *Rocket* was the first locomotive used on a public railway line

I. Industrial joint stock corporation of Paris

J. Cotton magnate and social reformer whose ideas contributed to the trade union movement

Choose the Correct Answer:

1. The Industrial Revolution in Britain was in large part inspired by

    a. the urgent need to solve severe urban poverty.
    b. the failure of the cottage industry system.
    c. entrepreneurs who sought and accepted new manufacturing methods and inventions.
    d. the great industrial success of the century before in Holland and France.
    e. mandates from royal officials such as Prince Albert.

2. The British industrial entrepreneur Richard Arkwright

    a. typified the well born, educated entrepreneurs of the Industrial Revolution.
    b. invented the water frame spinning machine.
    c. perfected the Crompton Mule.
    d. invented the steam locomotive.
    e. became a leading Member of Parliament.

3. James Watt invented the steam engine as a way to

    a. pump water from mines.
    b. weave cloth more efficiently.
    c. demonstrate his theories of motion.
    d. run the new locomotives.
    e. heat the Houses of Parliament.

4. The work ethic needed for efficient industrial production was taught as a religious virtue most noticeably in the

    a. Catholic monasteries of northern England.
    b. Lutheran gymnasia of western Germany.
    c. Jewish synagogues of Poland.
    d. Methodist meeting houses of the English midlands.
    e. Polytechnic institutes of the London area.

5. In the eighteenth century Britain's cotton industry

    a. could not keep pace with French textile production.
    b. was responsible for creating the first modern factories.
    c. declined due to the lack of technical innovations.
    d. went bankrupt due to gains in synthetic fiber production.
    e. built plants in several European cities.

6. The importance of railroads to the Industrial Revolution lay in the way they

    a. led to British supremacy in civil and mechanical engineering.
    b. increased the size of markets and the price of goods in those markets.
    c. brought an end to joint-stock companies.
    d. ended the need for domestically produced coal.
    e. enabled plant owners to live outside cities and commute to work.

7. The factory system and the values on which it was based were

    a. condemned by evangelical preachers as "unchristian."
    b. similar to those of the earlier cottage industry.
    c. successfully challenged by representatives of the working class.
    d. what relegated workers to lives of severe discipline and drudgery.
    e. proven to be inefficient and ineffective.

8. The Great Exhibition of 1851

    a. showed how the Industrial Revolution had achieved human domination over nature.
    b. displayed Britain's industrial wealth and might to the world.
    c. was housed in the Crystal Palace, itself a tribute to British engineering skills.
    d. was the brainchild of Prince Albert.
    e. all of the above

9. Industry on the continent differed from that in Britain because it

    a. used the private capital of rich individuals.
    b. used investments from joint-stock banks.
    c. invested in the latest equipment and most productive techniques.
    d. considered technical schools unnecessarily expensive.
    e. had a less dependable work force.

10. The Industrial Revolution in the United States

    a. never matched Britain's due to the lack of a system of internal transportation.
    b. employed large numbers of women in factories, especially in textile mills.
    c. utilized a labor-intensive system with many skilled workers.
    d. was limited mainly to the southern states.
    e. had less effect on social habits than that in Europe.

11. American industrialists overcame the problem of the country's vast size by

    a. building factories in every county of every state.
    b. manufacturing products that could be sold near factories.
    c. building roads, canals, and railroads.
    d. reducing tariffs between states.
    e. encouraging rapid urbanization.

12. American factory owners invested heavily in machinery because

    a. women and children were unable to do manual work.
    b. of the typically American fascination with gadgets.
    c. a skilled work force could use machines effectively.
    d. the American work force was largely unskilled.
    e. they were so much richer than their British counterparts.

13. In 1842 Edwin Chadwick published a landmark study of British

    a. poverty and urged greater sanitation.
    b. industrial profits and urged more mercantilism.
    c. schools and urged more instruction in ethics.
    d. fires and urged the use of asbestos in new housing.
    e. factory efficiency and urged shorter work hours.

14. The European population explosion of the nineteenth century

    a. can be explained by increased birthrates.
    b. was largely caused by the general disappearance of famine.
    c. was due to the absence of emigration.
    d. occurred despite the return of major epidemic diseases.
    e. was centered in the southern and eastern parts of the continent.

15. Mine workers during the industrial revolution

    a. were the best paid of common laborers.
    b. often moved up to jobs in factories.
    c. could be identified by their physical deformities.
    d. were the first to form recognized unions.
    e. appeared as heroes in early novels.

16. Which of these statements applies to European urban life in the early nineteenth century?

    a. Government intervention often prevented consumer fraud and food contamination.
    b. Healthier living conditions accounted for the increase in the urban population.
    c. Homes of urban workers were on the whole much nicer than those of farmers.
    d. Filthy sanitary conditions were exacerbated by the refusal of city authorities to take responsibility or action.
    e. As many people returned to the countryside each year as came into the cities.

17. The harsh treatment of children in the workplace during the early Industrial Revolution

    a. toughened and strengthened them physically for their adult lives.
    b. was not out of line with the brutal treatment of children in general.
    c. did not occur in mining because children were too small to work there.
    d. was often prevented by parish officials who employed children as pauper apprentices.
    e. increased after the Factory Act of 1833.

18. Before 1870 women's wages in textile mills were

    a. roughly the same as men's wages.
    b. paid directly to their husbands.
    c. half or less that of men's wages.
    d. paid only in food and clothing
    e. dependent upon their productivity.

19. The Luddites

    a. received strong support from the people they represented in Parliament.
    b. physically attacked machines they believed adversely affected their livelihood.
    c. were the lowest paid of unskilled workers in Great Britain.
    d. represented the first successful labor movement on the continent.
    e. were arrested and imprisoned for their crimes.

20. The "people's charter" demanded

    a. the right of all adult men to vote.
    b. that members of Parliament be paid for their services.
    c. the elimination of all property qualifications to run for office.
    d. annual sessions of Parliament.
    e. all of the above

Complete the Following Sentences:

1. Britain led the Industrial Revolution because it had deposits of _____ and _____, because it had abundant _____, and because of its small _____.

2. The cotton industry was pushed forward dramatically by the water frame spinning machine of Richard _____ and the power loom of Edmund _____.

3. Richard Trevithick pioneered the use of the steam-powered _____, but George Stephenson's _____ was the first used on a public line.

4. The Great Exhibition of 1851, held in the _____ _____ in _____, demonstrated that _____ led the world in industry.

5. Germany eventually played a major role in the industrial revolution because of _____ deposits in the _____ Valley of the _____.

6. In Ireland, where _____ peasants rented from absentee British _____ landlords, a mid-century _____ crop failure led to massive _____.

7. As secretary for the _____ _____ Commission, Edwin Chadwick blamed urban diseases on _____ impurities and called for reforms in _____.

8. Children were extensively used in factories because of their small _____, because they were easily _____ to work, and because they were a _____ supply of labor.

9. The People's Charter of 1838 demanded universal suffrage for _____, that Members of Parliament be _____, and that Parliament meet _____.

10. The Factory Acts passed between 1802 and 1819 limited child labor to _____ hours a day, forbade hiring of children under _____, and required that children be taught _____ and _____ during work hours.

Place the Following in Chronological Order and Give Dates:

1. Victoria and Albert's Great Exhibition   1.

2. People's Charter promulgated   2.

3. Cartwright invents the power loom   3.

4. Watt invents the rotary steam engine   4.

5. Ten Hours Act   5.

6. Trevithick first uses the steam locomotive   6.

7. Luddites attack machines   7.

Questions for Critical Thought

1. What prior conditions brought about the First Industrial Revolution, and why did it come first to Great Britain?

2. List the areas in which the Industrial Revolution enjoyed its most impressive successes. How did each field contribute to the overall pattern of technological progress?

3. Explain how and why the Great Exhibition of 1851 came to symbolize the Industrial Revolution and Britain's place in it.

4. Show how and why the Continental Industrial Revolution differed from that of Britain. Why did it eventually surpass the productivity of its island competitor?

5. Show how and why the Industrial Revolution in the United States differed from both the British and the Continental ones. What factors favored eventual American superiority?

6. Discuss the social impact (the effect on daily life) of the Industrial Revolution. Show how we are still today living with its social consequences.

7. Describe the lifestyle of the new industrial middle class. Compare it to that of the industrial workers. What were the results of the widening economic gap of the Nineteenth Century?

8. Discuss the various reactions to industrial abuses. What remedies were offered, by whom were they offered, and how successful were they?

Analysis of Primary Source Documents

1. List the traits Edward Baines said made Richard Arkwright a successful entrepreneur. Then list conditions, advantages, and probable personal traits that Baines failed to mention but which hindsight tells us also helped.

2. Describe the likely appearance and personality of a man or woman who had worked for five years under the rules of the Berlin Trading Company.

3. What commentary, hidden in his description of a steamship's arrival, was Mark Twain making about the effects on American life of the Industrial Revolution? Was he for it or against it?

4. Pretend you are one of the few British members of Parliament sympathetic to the Irish people and have just made a tour of their famine-stricken island. What would you demand that Parliament do?

5. What would you, a reform minded member of the British Parliament, have recommended the government do about child labor abuse? What would you have recommended as punishment for sadistic overseers?

6. Given the provocation they so often had, why do you suppose there were so few incidences of open rebellion among young industrial workers?

7. Although considered failures because they achieved no immediate results, what can you say of the Chartists' long-term and ultimate record?

CHAPTER TWENTY-ONE
REACTION, REVOLUTION, AND ROMANTICISM, 1815-1850

Chapter Outline

I. Conservative Order (1815-1830)
   A. Peace Settlement after Napoleon
      1. Restoration of Kingdoms
      2. Containment of France
   B. Ideology of Conservatism
      1. Edmund Burke's *Reflections* as Guide
      2. Joseph de Maistre's Order over Chaos
   C. Conservative Domination: Concert of Europe
      1. From Quadruple to Quintuple Alliance
      2. Intervention by the Great Powers
      3. Revolt in Latin America
      4. The Greek Revolt, 1821-1832
   D. The Conservative Domination: European States
      1. Rule of the Tories in Britain
         a. Peterloo
         b. Minor Reforms
      2. Bourbon Restoration in France
         a. Louis XVIII's Moderation
         b. Charles X and the Revolt of 1830
      3. Intervention in Italy and Spain
      4. Repression of Liberalism in Central Europe
         a. *Burschenschaften* Movement Thwarted in Germany
         b. Stagnation of Austria
      5. Tsarist Autocracy in Russia
         a. Promised Reforms
         b. The Decembrist Revolt
         c. The Reaction of Nicholas I

II. Ideologies of Change
   A. Liberalism
      1. Limitations on Government
         a. Thomas Malthus on Population
         b. David Ricardo on Wages
      2. Civil Liberties for the Individual
      3. Legislative Power over Monarchy
      4. John Stuart Mill and Women's Rights
   B. Nationalism
   C. Early Socialism
      1. The Phalansteries of Charles Fourier
      2. Robert Owen's New Lanark
      3. Louis Blanc and State Socialism
      4. Flora Tristan's Synthesis of Socialism and Feminism

III. Revolution and Reform, 1830-1850
    A.   Another French Revolution (1830)
        1.   The Middle Class Rule of Louis-Philippe
        2.   Parties of Movement and Resistance
    B.   Revolutionary Outbursts in Belgium, Poland, and Italy
    C.   Reform in Britain
        1.   Whig Reform Act of 1832
        2.   Repeal of the Corn Laws, in 1846
    D.   Revolutions of 1848
        1.   Yet Another French Revolution: Second Republic, Second Bonaparte
        2.   Frankfurt Assembly in Germany
        3.   Mazzini's *Risorgimento* in Italy
        4.   Failures of 1848
    E.   Growth of the United States
        1.   Jeffersonian Republicanism
        2.   John Marshall and National Unity
        3.   Mass Democracy of Jackson
        4.   Abolitionist Movement

IV. Emergence of an Ordered Society
    A.   New Police Forces
        1.   Louis-Maurice Debelleyme and Parisian *Serjents*
        2.   Robert Peel and London "Bobbies"
        3.   Berlin's *Schutzmannschaft*
    B.   Attacks on Poverty
    C.   Prison Reform

V. Culture in an Age of Reaction and Revolution: Romanticism
    A.   Characteristics of Romanticism
        1.   Sentiment and the Inner World: Example of Goethe
        2.   Individualism
        3.   Lure of the Middle Ages
        4.   Attraction to the Bizarre
    B.   Romantic Poets and the Love of Nature
        1.   Percy Bysshe Shelley
        2.   Lord Byron
        3.   William Wordsworth
    C.   Romanticism in Art and Music
        1.   Casper David Friedrich
        2.   William Turner
        3.   Eugene Delacroix
        4.   Ludwig van Beethoven
        5.   Hector Berlioz
    D.   Revival of Religion
        1.   Chateaubriand: Catholicism and the Harmony of All Things
        2.   Protestant Evangelicalism and Personal Salvation

Chapter Summary

The Congress of Vienna, which made peace at the end of the Napoleonic Wars, restored the Old Order and its "legitimate" rulers. It established a conservative system, with a balance of power, that the members hoped would give Europe peace as far as they could see into the future. Their scheme succeeded—for a time.

The conservative system was installed, but beneath a tranquil surface the barely suppressed ideals of liberty continued to stir up both hope and trouble. When combined with a rising call for independence and unification in nations long dependent and divided, it became a powerful agent of revolt and reform. Greece and the countries of Latin America threw off foreign masters. Revolts simmered and erupted finally in Russia, France, Austria, Germany, Belgium, Poland, and Italy. Some of them were successful, some were not; but together they made the first half of the nineteenth century a volatile time.

Intellectuals responded to the spirit of the times with various theories about human society. Edmund Burke defended conservatism as the best system to preserve the institutions that give society order and security, while John Stuart Mill argued that real order comes through the extension of individual freedom and while Louis Blanc held that governments should control the economy for the benefit of citizens. Some welcomed the continent-wide revolts of 1848, while some feared that political disintegration would soon follow, and perhaps both were surprised when the revolts led to more conservative regimes almost everywhere.

Yet reform did come, if not economic reform, certainly social. Police forces were created in major cities to keep order, and there were positive examples of prison reform. The reform movement had its cultural side, Romanticism, which brought forth a new generation of writers, artists, and musicians, all of them dedicated to a freedom previously unknown.

Learning Objectives

1. Be able to discuss the order which the victorious powers imposed upon post-Napoleonic Europe and why it was so successful for such a long period of time.

2. Describe the way the major powers dealt with liberal and nationalistic uprisings in various parts of the continent during the nineteenth century.

3. List the primary tenets of the liberalism that challenged the conservative establishment throughout the century, and determine how successful it was in the challenge.

4. Explain the reasons for and the consequences of the revolutions that swept the continent in 1830 and 1848.

5. Discuss the major assumptions and characteristics of Romanticism, and show how its various representatives affected literature, music, and art.

Glossary of Names and Terms

1. Edmund Burke: one of the nineteenth century's foremost political theorists, whose *Reflections on the Revolution in France* defended the conservative arguments for order.

2. Peterloo Massacre: name given to the suppression of a mass protest against grain prices in Manchester, England, where eleven people died at the hands of the British army.

3. Charles Fourier: utopian socialist whose proposals for social reform included the voluntary establishment of model cooperative communities.

4. Flora Tristan: early feminist who applied Fourier's ideas to the liberation and equality of women in cooperative communities.

5. Louis-Philippe: the "bourgeois" Duke of Orléans chosen to be King of France when the dictatorial Charles X was overthrown in 1830.

6. Giuseppe Mazzini: founder of Young Italy and intellectual guide to the movement toward nationalism in the Italian states.

7. Robert Peel: British Parliamentarian who introduced the bill that established the first police force for the city of London, for whom London police were often called Bobbies.

8. Romanticism: the early nineteenth century's cultural challenge to the Enlightenment's preoccupation with reason, shifting the emphasis to emotion.

9. Eugene Delacroix: most famous French Romantic artist, who combined a fascination with the exotic and a gift for dramatic coloration.

10. Beethoven: most famous Romantic composer, who broke with classical forms to adopt uncontrolled rhythms, dramatic struggles, and uplifted resolutions.

Match These Words with Their Definitions:

1. Bourbons

2. Edmund Burke

3. Whigs

4. Thomas Malthus

5. David Ricardo

6. Charles Fourier

7. July Revolution

8. "June Days"

9. Robert Peel

10. Eugene Delacroix

A. Party that attracted moneyed industrial groups

B. Advocated cooperative socialism to solve economic problems

C. Resulted in the overthrow of Louis-Philippe

D. Their restoration fulfilled Metternich's principle of legitimacy

E. Romantic artist with passion for color and exotic themes

F. Argued that wages rise only as population declines

G. Created London's Metropolitan Police Force

H. Spokesman for evolutionary conservatism

I. Resulted in the overthrow of Charles X

J. Argued that population growth mitigated against human progress

Choose the Correct Answer:

1. The Congress of Vienna

    a. gave Prussia complete control over Polish lands.
    b. sought to maintain a balance of power among members of the Quadruple Alliance.
    c. failed to achieve a long-lasting peace among the nations of Europe.
    d. treated France leniently, particularly after Napoleon's One Hundred Days.
    e. spent so much time in recreation that it overlooked many important issues.

2. Prince Klemens von Metternich

    a. supported the revolutionary ideology of the French philosophes.
    b. believed that a free press was necessary to maintain personal liberties.
    c. held that all European monarchs shared a common interest in stability.
    d. was an atheist who supported the suppression of religion.
    e. left the Congress of Vienna in disgust over its failures to adopt his resolutions.

3. The Quadruple Alliance became the Quintuple Alliance

    a. in 1818 with the addition of France.
    b. after the British Reform Act of 1832.
    c. in 1848 with the addition of Austria.
    d. after Italy became a nation in 1860.
    e. after Germany became a nation in 1870.

4. Conservatism, the political philosophy of European nations that defeated Napoleon

    a. was considered but rejected at Vienna as inappropriate for the new age.
    b. strongly supported the rights of the individual.
    c. was best defended by Edmund Burke in his *Reflections on the Revolution.*
    d. found no place in the work of the socialist Joseph de Maistre.
    e. slowly died away as rulers became more enlightened.

5. Within the Concert of Europe, Prince Metternich considered himself

    a. fire chief in a dry season.
    b. chief priest of a new nationalist religion.
    c. honorary emperor of an international empire.
    d. minister of police in a dangerous world.
    e. first citizen of a republican Europea.

6. The Concert of Europe was undoubtedly successful at

    a. ending the political domination of Greece by the Holy Alliance.
    b. thwarting Britain's attempts to intervene and crush revolts in Italy and Spain.
    c. crushing the colonial revolts in Latin America.
    d. all of the above
    e. none of the above

7.   The *Burschenschaften* (student societies of Germany) wanted to

    a.   spread the ideals of German nationalism and brotherhood.
    b.   dismantle the growing armed forces of Germany.
    c.   create a multi-ethnic European super state.
    d.   preserve the rights of German provinces.
    e.   assure that university graduates would lead the New Germany.

8.   The growing forces of liberalism and nationalism in central Europe were best characterized by the

    a.   reforms of Frederick William III in Prussia.
    b.   affinity and unity of ethnic groups under Frederick II of Austria.
    c.   liberal constitution adopted by the German Confederation in 1815.
    d.   the *Burschenschaften*, radical German student societies.
    e.   formation of a new Order of Catholic Socialists.

9.   Thomas Malthus argued that

    a.   food and population increase at approximately the same rates.
    b.   nature imposes restraints on the growth of population.
    c.   poverty is caused by absence of a work ethic among the poor.
    d.   economic growth depends upon a constant increase in population.
    e.   governments must intervene to assure public welfare.

10.   David Ricardo wrote that in order to overcome the "iron law of wages" governments should

    a.   establish cooperative gardens for urban workers.
    b.   do absolutely nothing because this was a law of nature.
    c.   create a bureau of employment to match men to jobs they were qualified to do.
    d.   send unemployable men to colonies in the Americas and Africa.
    e.   distribute free food and clothing on a regular basis.

11.   John Stuart Mill believed that women

    a.   should be honored as mothers of the race.
    b.   were both mentally and physically inferior to men.
    c.   could achieve as much as men if given proper educations.
    d.   should be given the vote after a proper period of education.
    e.   must use violence, if necessary, to gain their rights.

12.   Robert Owen achieved his greatest success in

    a.   New Lanark, Scotland, where he created a healthy utopian community.
    b.   New Harmony, Indiana, where a furniture factory made workers rich.
    c.   London, England, where he made a fortune in banking.
    d.   the West Indies, where his sugar mills gave work to thousands of poor people.
    e.   converting Parliament to his plan for cooperative economic zones.

13. The 1848 revolution in France resulted in

    a.   Louis-Philippe's acceptance of liberal reforms and survival as bourgeois monarch.
    b.   new elections for the National Assembly, resulting in a victory for republicans.
    c.   Europe's first socialist state under the guidance of phalansteries.
    d.   an authoritarian government ruled by Louis Napoleon.
    e.   national unity for Italy and Germany.

14. The German student response to the French Revolution of 1848 was one of

    a.   outrage and calls for war against France.
    b.   disbelief and despair over the coming chaos.
    c.   enthusiasm and optimism that Germany would be united.
    d.   joy that the French state was about to self-destruct.
    e.   pessimism for the Concert of Europe.

15. The social and political upheavals in central Europe through 1848-1849 led finally to

    a.   the failure of the Frankfurt Assembly in Germany.
    b.   an independent state for Hungary.
    c.   a united German-Austrian state patterned on the dreams of the *Grossdeutsch*.
    d.   the continued dominance of Metternich in Austria.
    e.   unity for the states of the Italian peninsula.

16. Young Italy was not

    a.   founded by the intellectual writer Giuseppe Mazzini.
    b.   in favor a united Italian Republic.
    c.   anti-religious and especially anti-Catholic.
    d.   a product of the *risorgimento* movement.
    e.   led both by men and women.

17. Compared to his counterparts in Paris and London, the nineteenth century Berlin police officer was better

    a.   dressed, with a uniform designed for maneuvers and pleasant appearance.
    b.   paid, with full sick leave and retirement benefits.
    c.   armed, with weapons that made him the equivalent of a soldier.
    d.   disciplined, with six weeks each summer spent at a training camp.
    e.   educated, equipped to deal with people who spoke different languages.

18. Goethe's *Sorrows of the Young Werther* reflects the Romantic obsession with

    a.   reforming the church, whether Catholic or Protestant.
    b.   creating nations with diverse ethnic populations.
    c.   bringing life to dead body parts.
    d.   maidens carried away young by disease.
    e.   gaining power by making contracts with Satan.

19. The Romantic poet Lord Byron

    a. lived the life of a medieval monk in an Anglican monastery.
    b. died while fighting for Greek independence.
    c. suggested to Mary Shelly the plot for her *Frankenstein.*
    d. retired to the Lake District with his sister when he was 55.
    e. probably died a virgin.

20. Among German Romantics there were

    a. more artists than in the Romantic Movement in other countries.
    b. fewer musicians than in the Romantic Movement in other countries.
    c. many more suicides than among Romantics elsewhere.
    d. attempts to introduce Indian mysticism to European thinkers.
    e. many conversions to the Catholic faith.

Complete the Following Sentences:

1.   At the Congress of Vienna, Austria's _____, guided by the principle of _____, sought to restore dynasties and create a _____ of power.

2.   With a weakened Spain unable to control the American colonies, _____ _____ led an army that gave many of them independence. The official position of the United States toward the new states, called the _____ _____ helped guarantee this independence.

3.   By the Treaty of Adrianople, Turkey agreed to let _____, _____, and _____ decide the fate of Greece. In 1830 they declared her _____.

4.   Following the _____ _____ against his accession, Russia's Nicholas I strengthened his _____ _____, making it a spy organization with sweeping powers.

5.   After the study of population growth by _____ _____ called into question the idea of human progress, the study of wages by _____ _____ called into question the power of any state to make man's life better.

6.   In order to create a better society, Charles Fourier advocated the establishment of voluntary economic communities called _____, and Robert Owen tried the idea in two places, successfully at _____ _____ in Scotland, unsuccessfully at _____ _____ in Indiana.

7.   Flora Tristan advocated a utopian synthesis of socialism and _____ in which men and women would live in _____ _____.

8.   The French Revolution of 1848 deposed the conservative king _____ _____ and established a Second Republic under President _____ _____ _____.

9.   The Metropolitan policemen of Paris, created under the leadership of Louis-Maurice _____, were called simply _____ and carried only a _____ by day and a _____ by night.

10. Romantic literature featured a range of subjects, from the Scottish historical novels of Sir
_____ _____ to the strange tale of *Frankenstein* by _____ _____.

Place the Following in Chronological Order and Give Dates:

1. Repeal of Corn Laws in Britain   1.

2. Decembrist Revolt in Russia   2.

3. July Revolution in France   3.

4. Beginning of Greek revolt against the Turks   4.

5. British Reform Act   5.

6. Revolts or revolutions in France, Germany, Italy, and Austria   6.

7. Beginning of Wars of Independence in Latin America   7.

Questions for Critical Thought

1. Outline the social and political world of Europe that emerged from the decisions of the Congress of Vienna. How did it seek to establish a balance of power? Why is it called a Monument to Conservatism?

2. Explain the ideology of nineteenth-century Conservatism, and show how it both dominated and provoked reaction during the period from 1815 to 1848.

3. List all the revolts against the "Bourbon" monarchies between the years 1815 and 1848. What were their common causes, and what did they generally achieve?

4. Compare and contrast the period 1815-1870 in Britain and in France. Account for the different set of events and final results.

5. List the intellectual bases on which the various movements against Conservatism were mounted. Explain how each one contributed to the desire for and belief in change.

6. Describe the Revolutions of 1848, where they occurred, who led them, what they hoped to achieve, and how each one ended.

7. What effects did the Conservative Age have on daily life in Europe? What effects did the Liberal era that followed it have? In what sense were these two sides of a single coin?

8. Define Romanticism. Discuss its characteristics, its major representatives, the various fields of the arts it affected, and what its lasting achievements were.

Analysis of Primary Source Documents

1. According to Austria's Prince Metternich, what characteristics of a nation give its people security and stability? Explain how he feels each characteristic contributes to the whole.

2. What did the German university student of 1845 dream of accomplishing? How did he distinguish himself from his father's generation? How realistic were his goals?

3. How do John Stuart Mill's views on "liberty" reflect the death of an old world and the birth of a new one? How will such ideas be tested in this new century of ours?

4. Explain in simplest terms Macaulay's argument for the Reform Act of 1832. Show why he is considered one of the greatest of pragmatic thinkers.

5. Describe the enthusiasm of young German liberals like Carl Schurz when they believed their long-awaited revolution was at hand. Suggest three probable reactions among such young people when they realized it had failed.

6. Outline the "doctrine" of nineteenth-century Nationalism as illustrated by the Young Italy Oath. How and to what degree was it, as some have argued, a form of secular religion?

7. What complaints did London police of the 1840s make about their working conditions? How effectively did their petition communicate their complaints? Explain.

8. Explain the nineteenth century's love for "Gothic" literature, particularly its tendency to combine romance and horror, as illustrated by the writings of Edgar Allen Poe. What does this say about the age—and the Romantic Movement?

CHAPTER TWENTY-TWO
AN AGE OF NATIONALISM AND REALISM, 1850-1871

Chapter Outline

I. France of Napoleon III
   A. Louis Napoleon as President
      1. Winning Support
      2. Election as Emperor
   B. Second Napoleonic Empire
      1. Stimulating the Economy
      2. Rebuilding Paris
      3. Liberalization
      4. Foreign Policy: Mexico and the Crimean War

II. National Unification Movements
   A. Unification of Italy
      1. House of Savoy and Victor Emmanuel II
      2. Camillo di Cavour
      3. Garibaldi and his Red Shirts
      4. Unification (1861)
      5. Rome (1770)
   B. Unification of Germany
      1. William I Hohenzollern
      2. Otto von Bismarck and *Realpolitik*
      3. Danish War (1864)
      4. Austro-Prussian War (1866)
      5. Franco-Prussian War (1870-1871)
      6. Unification (1871)

III. Nation Building and Reform: National States at Mid-Century
   A. Austrian Empire
      1. Francis Joseph and the Dual Monarchy
      2. Domination by Germans and Magyars
   B. Imperial Russia
      1. Alexander II and the Emancipation of the Serfs
      2. *Zemstvos* Assemblies
      3. Alexander Herzen and Populism
   C. Britain's Victorian Age
      1. Palmerston's Conservatism
      2. Disraeli and the Reform of 1867
      3. Gladstone and the Liberal Party
   D. United States: Civil War and Reunion
   E. Emergence of a Canadian Nation

IV. Industrialization and the Marxist Response
   A.   Industrialization on the Continent
      1.   Less Barriers to International Trade
      2.   Weak Trade Unions
   B.   Marx and Marxism
      1.   Life and Experience of Karl Marx
      2.   *The Communist Manifesto*
      3.   Bourgeoisie and Proletariat
      4.   Classless Society

V.   Science and Culture in an Age of Realism
   A.   New Age of Science
      1.   Proliferation of Discoveries
      2.   Faith in Science's Benefits
   B.   Darwin and the Theory of Evolution
      1.   Trip of the *Beagle*
      2.   "Natural Selection"
   C.   Revolution in Health Care
      1.   Pasteur and Lister
      2.   Medical Training
      3.   Women in Medicine
   D.   Auguste Comte's Positivism
   E.   Realism in Literature and Art
      1.   Realistic Novel
         a.   Gustave Flaubert
         b.   William Thackeray
         c.   Charles Dickens
      2.   Realism in Art
         a.   Gustave Courbet
         b.   Jean-Francois Millet
   F.   Music: Twilight of Romanticism
      1.   Franz Liszt
      2.   Richard Wagner

Chapter Summary

Just after the midpoint of the nineteenth century, the suppressed emotions that had constantly bubbled for three decades finally erupted. The nations of Europe spent their energies in unification or reform; and the result affected Western development for the next century.

The memories of Napoleonic greatness which had haunted France saw fulfillment with first the election as president and then the proclamation as emperor of Napoleon's nephew, who took the grand title Emperor Napoleon III. From 1852, until he was deposed in 1870, Napoleon made and unmade policy across the continent and even meddled in the affairs of the New World. The dreams of Mazzini were fulfilled when Cavour and Garibaldi, working sometimes at odds, succeeded in unifying Italy for the first time since the fall of the Roman Empire. Under the guidance of Bismarck, Prussia maneuvered and fought its way to the head of a unified German Empire. In Russia and the United States, serfs and slaves were freed, in the former by imperial decree, in the latter by constitutional amendment. And in Britain the pressures of industrialization forced a series of reforms that made the realm of Queen Victoria a bit more democratic.

Science continued to make discoveries and to change life both socially and personally. Yet while health care greatly improved with discoveries about bacteria and infection, more and more workers fell into what Marx called the "wage slavery" of the industrial market. While political leaders like Disraeli and Gladstone believed that justice could be achieved by reform, Marx held that only a revolution of the workers would bring about a classless society. Both the *realpolitik* of nations and the realities of industrial life affected the arts, ushering in a new era of Realism. The world was often brutal and grim, and writers and artists portrayed it with pitiless accuracy.

Learning Objectives

1. Be able to describe the rise of Louis Napoleon and explain why and how he was able to have such an influence on France at the middle of the nineteenth century.

2. Trace the progress of the movement to unify Italy, explaining the effects of ideology, personality, and fortune in its final success.

3. Trace the progress of the movement to unify Germany, explaining the effects of ideology, personality, and fortune in its final success.

4. Explain Karl Marx's motives and methods as he wrote his books, and account for his certainty that he knew the future.

5. Describe the advances in science during the middle and later nineteenth century, and show how these advances affected European society, including culture.

Glossary of Names and Terms

1. Baron Haussmann: engineer who, under Napoleon III, planned and carried out the reconstruction of the city of Paris.

2. Victor Emmanuel II: King of Piedmont who, with the guidance of Count Cavour and military prowess of Garibaldi, became the first King of a united Italy.

3. Red Shirts: the volunteer army of Garibaldi, which brought the southern half of the Italian peninsula into the new nation.

4. Bismarck: civil servant of the Junker class who became prime minister of Prussia and used his sometimes devious skills to unify the German nation.

5. Benjamin Disraeli: Tory prime minister of Great Britain who sponsored the Reform Bill of 1867 and thus move directly toward full democratization of the country.

6. *Das Kapital*: the work in which Karl Marx explained his view of the capitalist system and offered his plan for the classless society.

7. H.M.S. Beagle: the ship in which Charles Darwin sailed around the world, collecting scientific samples that would give examples of his theory of evolution.

8. Elizabeth Blackwell: the first American woman to complete medical training and serve as a doctor, eventually running her own New York clinic.

9. Auguste Comte: author of *System of Positive* Philosophy, he was a leading voice in the movement to apply the principles of scientific research to the study of human society.

10. William Thackeray: author of *Vanity Fair: A Novel without a Hero*, one of the major works of the literature of Realism.

Match These Words with Their Definitions:

1. Camillo di Cavour

2. Giuseppe Garibaldi

3. Benjamin Disraeli

4. William Gladstone

5. Dialectical Materialism

6. Michael Faraday

7. Louis Pasteur

8. Joseph Lister

9. Positivism

10. Gustave Flaubert

A. Conservative prime minister who passed the Reform Bill of 1867

B. How economic forces will bring a classless society

C. Auguste Comte's theory that only scientifically verified facts are valid

D. Using carbolic acid, he eliminated surgical infections

E. Prime Minister who helped make Victor Emmanuel King of Italy

F. Builder of the first generator of electricity

G. Perfecter of the realist novel with his *Madame Bovary*

H. Military leader who added Sicily to the new Kingdom of Italy

I. Chemist who pioneered in fermentation and bacteriology

J. Liberal prime minister who introduced the secret ballot

Choose the Correct Answer:

1. In establishing the Second Empire, Napoleon III

    a. received the overwhelming support of the people.
    b. granted the National Assembly stronger powers.
    c. rescinded universal male suffrage.
    d. cared little about public opinion.
    e. destroyed the Concert of Europe.

2. During the 1860s the more liberal Napoleon III

    a. legalized trade unions and permitted them to strike.
    b. allowed candidates opposed to his regime to campaign for office.
    c. permitted the legislative corps more say in affairs of state.
    d. opened the budget to public debate.
    e. all of the above

3. Napoleon III chose Baron Haussmann to direct the rebuilding of

    a. the French National Assembly.
    b. Charlemagne's ancient capital of Aix-la-Chapelle.
    c. major historical churches throughout France.
    d. the entire city of Paris.
    e. Versailles, so that he could use it as his residence.

4. The Crimean War convinced Napoleon III that he had an international mission to

    a. champion movements for national independence.
    b. spread liberalism throughout Europe.
    c. referee continental disputes.
    d. contain the military ambitions of Russia.
    e. place his cousin on the throne of Mexico.

5. One result of the Crimean War was

    a. the perpetuation of the Concert of Europe until 1914.
    b. continued Russian expansionism into Europe for the next two decades.
    c. increased British involvement in continental affairs.
    d. an international climate in which both Italian and German unification were possible.
    e. an international call for a Jewish state.

6. As leader of the Italian unification movement, Camillo di Cavour

    a. stoked the Piedmont economy in order to pay for a large army.
    b. personally led Italian troops against Austria.
    c. sent Italian troops to support Prussia against Austria in 1866.
    d. considered Napoleon III to be Italy's most bitter enemy.
    e. voluntarily retired at the same time Garibaldi did.

7. Before the administration of Bismarck, a prime characteristic of the Prussian state was that

    a. William I had little concern for the deterioration of his army.
    b. the wealthiest men controlled the most seats in parliament.
    c. the middle class had no voice in either house of parliament.
    d. Parliament could not reject a royal proposal.
    e. there was no clear line of succession to the throne.

8. A result of Bismarck's Austro-Prussian War was that

    a. Austria became a member of the North German Confederation.
    b. Austria was reduced to the level of a second-rate power.
    c. liberal Prussians spoke out against Bismarck's expansionist policies.
    d. France welcomed a unified Germany on its eastern border.
    e. none of the above

9. The immediate cause of the Franco-Prussian War was

    a. the ascent of a French prince to the Spanish throne.
    b. Napoleon III's reaction to the telegram Bismarck edited.
    c. the French invasion of Alsace-Lorraine.
    d. Napoleon III's annexation of Schleswig-Holstein.
    e. Bismarck's public insult of Napoleon III.

10. The creation of the dual monarchy of Austria-Hungary

    a. allowed Magyars and German-speaking Austrians to dominate ethnic minorities.
    b. enabled Alexander von Bach to become an absolute dictator.
    c. gave Hungary independence in its domestic affairs.
    d. overturned the Compromise of 1867.
    e. was first proposed by Napoleon III.

11. In the 1860s Russia and the United States both

    a. experienced devastating civil wars.
    b. saw radical liberals assassinate high government officials.
    c. fought unsuccessful wars against Britain.
    d. emancipated enslaved populations within their borders.
    e. intervened in the domestic affairs of neighboring countries.

12. As British Prime Minister from 1855 to 1865, Lord Palmerston

    a. instituted universal male suffrage.
    b. staunchly opposed extending the franchise.
    c. defended the interests of the working class.
    d. instituted competitive examinations for the civil service.
    e. worked to allow Catholics the right to sit in Parliament.

13. A central goal of Disraeli's domestic agenda in Britain was

    a. winning the working classes to the Tory Party.
    b. extending the franchise to women.
    c. laying minor taxes on the royalty.
    d. sending more middle class students to Oxford and Cambridge.
    e. recognizing and increasing the power of trade unions.

14. Continental industrial growth between1850 to 1870 lay largely in the

    a. production of iron, as Germany surpassed Britain.
    b. complete replacement of hand looms with electrically powered ones.
    c. rapid expansion of the railroad system across the continent.
    d. replacement of charcoal with coke as the chief agent of factory fuel.
    e. continued slow development of American industry.

15. In Karl Marx's vision of the industrial future, the political state would

    a. be violently torn apart in class warfare.
    b. wither away because it would no longer be unnecessary.
    c. dominate every part of the citizen's life.
    d. be made much more efficient through technological bureaucracy.
    e. continue to be the irrelevant plaything of the idle rich.

16. Scientific discoveries and advances during the nineteenth century led to all of the following *except*

    a. a renewal of religious faith and spiritual commitment.
    b. the contention that material reality was the only reality.
    c. great advances in mathematics and thermodynamics.
    d. inventions that affected everyone's daily life.
    e. new controversies about the origin of man.

17. Which of the following best applies to Charles Darwin and his evolutionary theory?

    a. He argued that advantageous variants determine survival.
    b. His *Origin of Species* traced man's evolution from animal to human.
    c. He wrote the first rational version of the theory of evolution.
    d. His ideas were accepted by religious leaders because they made man the crown of creation.
    e. He won many skeptics to his theories with his polished and erudite lectures.

18. Elizabeth Blackwell earned the first medical degree in the United States

    a. the year Lincoln was elected president.
    b. by a combination of admission error and perseverance.
    c. despite a petition opposing her graduation by male students.
    d. with the strong support of the president of the A.M.A.
    e. as the ward of heiress Harriet Hunt.

19. The literary Realists of the mid-nineteenth century

    a. avoided the imagery of the Romantic Dickens.
    b. employed emotional language to encourage religious renewal.
    c. preferred ordinary characters to mythic heroes.
    d. actively took part in social protest movements.
    e. featured women in their works more than the Romantics had done.

20. Realist painters

    a. earned the praise of critics for showing the beauty of common people.
    b. followed the example of Millet and emphasized urban squalor.
    c. earned more money than artists of any other school.
    d. demonstrated a particular interest in the natural environment.
    e. all came from the lower class.

Complete the Following Sentences:

1. With the disintegration of the _____ Empire, Russia tried to carve out a new sphere of influence, only to be attacked in its _____ Peninsula by France and _____, destroying the old _____ of Europe.

2. Garibaldi, a republican believer in Mazzini's _____ movement, was finally persuaded to accept an Italian kingdom under King _____ _____ of the house of _____.

3. In order to achieve German unification, Bismarck successfully went to war against _____, _____, and _____, the latter ending with the proclamation of the German _____.

4. Alexander II's Emancipation Edict allowed former Russian serfs to own _____, _____ whom they chose, and bring lawsuits; but resentment against the limits of freedom led to Alexander's _____ in 1881.

5. Although the British Liberal Party led in calls for voting reform, the Reform Bill of 1867 was passed under the leadership of the Conservative Prime Minister _____ _____. In the next election, the _____ Party won a huge victory.

6. Karl Marx, descended from a line of _____ _____, was raised in the _____ faith but was denied a professorship because of his avowed _____.

7. Marx and Engels claimed in their _____ _____ that a class war would end with the complete victory of _____ over _____ and a _____ society.

8. Building upon his South Sea findings, Charles Darwin discarded the notion of _____ creationism in favor of the principle of _____ _____.

9. Flaubert's realist novel *Madame Bovary* tells of a provincial woman inspired by _____ stories to experiment with _____, only to end up a _____, yet unrepentant.

10. Richard Wagner helped realize the nationalist dream of a truly _____ opera, using ancient myths to write his *Ring of the* _____, four operas based upon an ancient German _____.

Place the Following in Chronological Order and Give Dates:

1. Tories pass British Reform Act   1.

2. American Civil War ends   2.

3. Second Empire proclaimed in France   3.

4. Italy annexes Rome   4.

5. German Empire proclaimed   5.

6. Austro-Prussian War   6.

7. Russian Emancipation Edict   7.

Questions for Critical Thought

1. Describe the Second French Empire. How did it come about, what were its domestic characteristics, what were its foreign policies, and how did it end?

2. Describe the unification of Italy. Show how men and historical circumstances cooperated to achieve the dream of *risorgimento*.

3. Explain how Bismarck accomplished the unification of Germany. What kind of legacy did he thereby leave his people and nation?

4. Discuss the progress made during the second half of the nineteenth century by the nations already unified by 1850. Show how "the liberal agenda" fared in each one.

5. Explain the theories of Karl Marx. What circumstances, political and personal, led him to them? Why would they so strongly appeal to radical reformers?

6. What did the second age of scientific discovery add to human knowledge? Was it more "practical" than the earlier age? Explain.

7. Define the term "Realism" as applied to the literature and art of the late nineteenth century. Give examples of it, and show its legacy to our own day.

8. What progress was made in professional medicine in the late nineteenth century? How did women break into the profession? Give examples.

Analysis of Primary Source Documents

1. Explain how Louis Napoleon used the high ideal of national well being to forward his goal of personal power. In what ways was he a model for twentieth-century dictators?

2. Describe the newspaper account of Garibaldi's walk through war-torn Palermo. Then write the story as a twenty-first century reporter would tell it.

3. Explain how Bismarck "edited" his king's telegram from Ems to make the French feel they had been insulted. What was his purpose in doing this, and how well did he succeed?

4. Compare and contrast the emancipation proclamations of Tsar Alexander II and Abraham Lincoln. Which was the more thorough and why?

5. Having read Marx's description of the way industrial society will arrive at the classless society, how would you describe Marx's opinion of man's nature?

6. Why did Darwin's theory of man's origins cause such a stir? What did nineteenth century Britons find offensive and attractive about it?

7. Describe the first use of ether in surgery. How do you account for the writer's hyperbole?

8. What made Charles Dickens' description of industrial Birmingham so powerful? What does his portrayal say about his own feelings on the subject?

Map Exercise 12

MAP EXERCISE 12: THE UNIFICATION OF GERMANY AND ITALY

Shade and label the following:

Germany

1. Alsace
2. Baden
3. Bavaria
4. East Prussia
5. Hanover
6. Hesse
7. Lorraine
8. Oldenburg
9. Schleswig-Holstein
10. West Prussia
11. Württemburg

Italy

1. Lombardy
2. Modena
3. Papal States
4. Parma
5. Piedmont
6. Romagna
7. Savoy
8. Tuscany
9. Two Sicilies
10. Umbria
11. Venezia

Pinpoint and label the following:

Germany

1. Berlin
2. Frankfurt
3. Leipzig
4. Munich
5. Strasbourg
6. Trier
7. Weimar

Italy

1. Florence
2. Genoa
3. Milan
4. Naples
5. Rome
6. Turin
7. Venice

CHAPTER TWENTY-THREE
THE MASS SOCIETY IN AN "AGE OF PROGRESS," 1871-1894

Chapter Outline

I.   Growth of Industrial Prosperity
    A.   New Products and New Markets
        1.   The Substitution of Steel for Iron
        2.   Electricity, the New Source of Energy
        3.   Internal Combustion Engine
    B.   New Markets
        1.   Cartels and Larger Factories
        2.   Tariffs
    C.   New Patterns in an Industrial Economy
        1.   Depression to Prosperity
        2.   Germany Surpasses Britain
        3.   Union of Science and Technology
        4.   European Economic Zones
        5.   A World Economy
    D.   Women and New Job Opportunities
        1.   Sweatshops
        2.   White Collar Work
        3.   Prostitution and Lower Class Women
    E.   Organizing the Working Class
        1.   Socialist Parties
        2.   Revisions of Marxist Thought
            a.   Evolution, Not Revolution
            b.   Divisiveness of Nationalism
        3.   Role of Trade Unions
        4.   Anarchist Alternative

II. Emergence of Mass Society
    A.   Population Growth and Emigration
        1.   Improved Public Sanitation
        2.   An Improved Diet
        3.   Increased Emigration
    B.   Transformation of the Urban Environment
        1.   Growth of Cities
        2.   Improving Living Conditions
            a.   Sanitation
            b.   Housing
        3.   Redesigning the Cities
    C.   Social Structure of Mass Society
        1.   Elite: Wealth and Status
        2.   Middle Classes: Good Conduct
        3.   Lower Classes: Skilled, Semiskilled, and Unskilled

    D. Role of Women
      1. Cult of Domesticity
      2. Birth Control
      3. Middle Class Family
      4. Working Class Family
    E. Education in an Age of Mass Society
      1. Primary Education for All
        a. For A More Efficient Work Force
        b. For A More Intelligent Electorate
      2. Demand for Teachers
      3. Increase in Literacy
    F. Mass Leisure
      1. Dance Halls
      2. Tourism
      3. Sports

III. National State
    A. Western Europe: Growth of Political Democracy
      1. British Reform
      2. France's Third Republic
      3. Parliamentary Government in Spain
      4. Italy's Instability
    B. Central and Eastern Europe: Persistence of the Old Order
      1. Germany: Bismarck's Conservatism
      2. Austria's Imperial Decrees
      3. Absolutism in Russia

Chapter Summary

After 1871 the nations of Europe were preoccupied for a quarter century with achieving true national unity, adjusting to the economics of a second industrial revolution, and adapting to the realities of rapid urbanization. Despite the rise and acceleration of international rivalries and animosities, they were simply too busy to fight among themselves.

During this period inventions based on steel, electricity, and the internal combustion engine led to a new industrial economy which changed the nature of markets and created a true world economy. Women found new opportunities for gainful employment, yet they were also often seduced into rings of subservience and prostitution. Socialist parties, with a more moderate form of Marxism, began organizing for action through trade unionism and political action. Europe suffered the birth pangs of a new age.

Mass Society was born. The European population increased dramatically through better sanitation and diet, yet emigration prevented overcrowding. Class divisions continued to dictate styles of living, and women of the upper strata were encouraged to pursue a cult of domesticity, yet this age also saw the dawn of female consciousness and of birth control. The amount and quality of education increased in order to provide a better-trained work force and a more intelligent voting public, and there arose more opportunities to enjoy life through leisure activities. The European nations moved in two opposite directions. In Britain and France liberal parties increased democratic participation in government, while in Germany, Austria, and especially Russia, monarchs held to their powers with stubborn abandon. The times were changing, but it was not clear what the looming new century would bring.

Learning Objectives

1. Be able to describe the Second Industrial Revolution and show how it was different from the First Industrial Revolution.

2. Discuss the characteristics of the nineteenth century working class and how it related to national political parties.

3. Describe the way the Second Industrial Revolution changed the urban environment and thus the lives of urban dwellers.

4. Trace the development of education and leisure activities in the new urban environment and how these affected nineteenth century families.

5. Compare and contrast political developments in the western and eastern parts of the continent, and explain why they were so different.

Glossary of Names and Terms

1. Guglielmo Marconi: typifying the inventors of the Second Industrial Revolution, he succeeded in sending radio waves across the Atlantic in 1901.

2. Gottlieb Daimler: a pioneer in the development of the internal combustion engine, his lighter model ushered in the era of the automobile.

3. Eduard Bernstein: a German socialist whose years of exile in England persuaded him that socialism would be stronger if brought to power through popular vote.

4. Michael Bakunin: Russian anarchist who believed that small cells of fanatical revolutionaries could bring down governments.

5. Consuelo Vanderbilt: wealthy American heiress whose marriage to the British Duke of Marlborough epitomized the social merger of aristocrats and plutocrats.

6. Aletta Jacobs: signaled the change in attitudes toward women's rights, she established the first birth control clinic in Amsterdam in 1882.

7. Robert Baden-Powell: founder of the Boy Scouts of Britain in 1908, who also encouraged his sister to establish a similar organization for girls.

8. Thomas Cook: secretary to a British temperance organization, he learned to arrange low priced holiday tours, first in England and then to the continent.

9. Rugby Union: one of the earliest professional sports organizations, based on a game originated at the Rugby School in England.

10. *Kulturkampf*: the word Bismarck used to describe his attack first on Catholics and later on socialists, both of whom he said were enemies of the German state.

Match These Words with Their Definitions:

1. Rudolf Virchow

2. Octavia Hill

3. Bertha Krupp

4. Consuelo Vanderbilt

5. Agnes Baden-Powell

6. Barbara Bodichon

7. Thomas Cook

8. William Gladstone

9. Paris Commune

10. *Kulturkampf*

A. British founder of the Guides

B. Organizer of Temperance trips

C. Wealthiest woman in Germany at the turn of this century

D. Violently crushed in 1871

E. American who married into British royalty

F. Advocate of urban sanitation reform

G. Failed in an attempt to limit Catholic power

H. Pioneer in the field of female education

I. Worked to provide homes for the poor

J. Advocate of Irish Home Rule

Choose the Correct Answer:

1. Which of the following statements is false?

   a. Henry Ford produced the first light engine.
   b. Marconi sent the first radio waves across the Atlantic.
   c. Alexander Graham Bell invented the telephone.
   d. Joseph Swan invented the light bulb.
   e. The Zeppelin was the first successful air transport.

2. Cartels were designed primarily to

   a. enrich nation states.
   b. raise funds for social programs.
   c. restrain competition that lowered prices.
   d. provide police protection for companies.
   e. distribute low cost milk and food containers.

3. Working-class men most often used which of these arguments to try to keep women out of industrial work?

   a. Keeping them at home made for stronger families.
   b. They were physically too weak to do the work.
   c. It was not God's will for them to work.
   d. They were already too politically active.
   e. The jobs they would take would diminish the kind of jobs men did best.

4. Most large-city prostitutes were

    a. wives bringing in extra money for their families.
    b. dead by the age of 30 from disease.
    c. regularly herded into churches for public rebuke.
    d. active for only a short time and went on to other work or marriage.
    e. registered with local police and health clinics.

5. Edward Bernstein stressed the need to

    a. use violence to overthrow capitalist governments.
    b. assassinate corrupt governmental officials.
    c. work within political systems to achieve socialism.
    d. adhere strictly to all Marxist doctrines.
    e. keep party membership roles totally secret.

6. Annual emigration from Europe to America

    a. more than doubled from 1880 to 1900.
    b. leveled off after the1890 census.
    c. had no positive benefits to European society.
    d. contained almost no Jews.
    e. led to riots in New York and Boston in 1895.

7. The most successful of the public health legislative acts were

    a. passed in Poland and Russia, where they were most needed.
    b. the ones that created boards of health that worked for reforms.
    c. lucky to solve as many problems as they created.
    d. condemned by church officials as socialistic.
    e. actively opposed by socialists and communists.

8. Octavia Hill's housing venture was designed to

    a. provide luxurious urban housing for the new rich classes.
    b. give charity to the helpless and hopeless poor.
    c. let the wealthy experience poverty for a week each year.
    d. break down class barriers in preparation for a socialist state.
    e. give the poor an environment in which to improve themselves.

9. Experiments in public housing proved that

    a. government housing was doomed to failure.
    b. poor people would not keep their premises sanitary.
    c. such projects needed private monies to keep them afloat.
    d. governments must construct houses on a grand scale.
    e. there would always be inequities in living conditions.

10. The marriage of the Duke of Marlborough to a wealthy heiress

    a.   showed the newly acquired influence of the Krupp family.
    b.   set the stage for the Prince of Wales to marry a commoner.
    c.   illustrated the practical merger of the aristocrats with the plutocrats.
    d.   ended in divorce before it produced an heir.
    e.   meant that future prime minister Winston Churchill would not be a lord.

11. The wealthy elite of the new industrial age

    a.   came to be dominated by upper-middle-class families with fortunes made in industry.
    b.   consisted mostly of landed aristocracy.
    c.   controlled only slightly more total wealth than did all the working class.
    d.   was more open to admission by newcomers in Russia than in any other country.
    e.   elected themselves to Parliament from pocket boroughs.

12. In 1882, Dr. Aletta Jacob opened Europe's first

    a.   housing unit for female industrial workers in London.
    b.   birth control clinic in Amsterdam.
    c.   abortion clinic in Glasgow.
    d.   home for unwed mothers in Berlin.
    e.   catholic boarding school for working class girls.

13. The middle classes of late nineteenth-century Europe

    a.   were composed of shopkeepers and manufacturers who barely lived above the property line.
    b.   offered almost no opportunity for their women to improve themselves through education.
    c.   were extremely concerned with propriety and adhered to values of hard work and Christian morality.
    d.   viewed the idea of progress with extreme distrust and went out of their way not to be a part of it.
    e.   led the way in Parliaments to bring social programs to the working classes.

14. The domestic ideal of the late nineteenth-century middle class family was

    a.   each member holding a job so as to increase the overall family income.
    b.   spending time together, especially at leisure activities.
    c.   a strict, almost military command by the father.
    d.   for boys to be educated for careers and girls to be married as early as possible.
    e.   that at least one child go abroad and return with money for investment.

15. Changes in the standard of living from 1890 to 1914 affected the working-class family

    a.   positively because with more children working the family income increased.
    b.   negligibly because most families could still not afford consumer products.
    c.   negatively because real income were severely reduced.
    d.   positively because working-class mothers could devote more time to child rearing.
    e.   negatively because usually one daughter had to go into prostitution.

16. The motive for mass education is believed to have been political because

   a. the expansion of voting rights demanded a more enlightened electorate.
   b. politicians could win votes by promising more money for education.
   c. contractors who built school buildings had political clout.
   d. many schools specialized in training government officials.
   e. the Tories knew that the more education a person had the more conservative he was.

17. Music and dance hall were obviously designed and operated for

   a. an upper-class audience who liked to "slum" in poor neighborhoods.
   b. soldiers on leave from their duties or from nearby barracks.
   c. an audience that was chiefly working class and male.
   d. the benefit of West End theaters, which drew their talent from such training grounds.
   e. the moral benefit of people who might otherwise fall into sin.

18. The Second French Empire was at last replaced by a

   a. monarchy, declared to be the "only true French regime."
   b. Third Empire, under Napoleon IV.
   c. Communist regime, allied with Soviet Russia.
   d. Third Republic, which was overwhelmingly popular from the start.
   e. Third Republic, which survived despite severe internal divisions.

19. Which statement best applies to Germany under the chancellorship of Otto von Bismarck?

   a. Prussia lost much of its military edge against its neighbors.
   b. Bismarck used coalitions until they accomplished their purposes, then dropped them.
   c. The army stamped out almost all vestiges of civilian socialism.
   d. All regional differences disappeared under Bismarck's conciliatory hand.
   e. Germany came to feel secure against all threats, foreign and domestic.

20. Which of these statements best applies to the Dual Monarchy of Austria-Hungary?

   a. Both Austria and Hungary had parliamentary systems.
   b. The Magyars dominated the empire as long as William II reigned.
   c. Ethnic tensions remained unresolved and contributed to feelings of insecurity among the German ruling class.
   d. Prime Minister Count Eduard von Taafe was ousted in 1893 by Slavic minorities for failing to satisfy their demands.
   e. The line of succession was made secure when Francis Ferdinand married a princess of Denmark.

Complete the Following Sentences:

1. British industrialists fell behind their _____ counterparts because they were suspicious of _____ and failed to invest in _____ education.

2. Women first broke into the labor force because of the increased importance of _____ _____ work, which generally required few skills beyond literacy. The only women's careers that demanded more were _____ and _____.

3. French socialism differed from socialism in other countries because it looked not to
    _____ ideology but to the _____ _____ experience for its inspiration and
    direction.

4. Rapid urbanization meant that while in 1800 there were _____ European cities over 100,000 in
    population, by 1900 there were _____. During the same time period England's urban population
    went from _____ to _____ percent.

5. In England _____ and _____ were the first cities to have town councils build public
    housing, after concluding that _____ _____ could not do all that was needed for
    the working classes.

6. Even though vulcanized rubber made possible the manufacture of _____ and _____
    by 1850, they were not widely used for birth control until much later. Some historians believe that
    women at times limited the number of children by _____.

7. Liberals hoped that mass education would provide average citizens with _____ and
    _____ training based on positive _____ values.

8. The independent Parisian republic called the _____ was ended when 20,000 people were
    _____ and 10,000 shipped to a _____ _____.

9. The _____ officers of the German army believed it their duty to defend
    _____ and _____; and their general staff answered only to the _____.

10. The paranoid Russian Emperor Alexander III greatly expanded the powers of his
    _____ _____ and placed entire districts under _____ _____.

Place the Following in Chronological Order and Give Dates:

1. Bismarck's antisocialist law   1.

2. Bernstein's *Evolutionary Socialism* published   2.

3. Nicholas II becomes tsar   3.

4. The new Spanish constitution   4.

5. The Paris Commune   5.

6. Aletta Jacob opens her clinic in Amsterdam   6.

7. British Housing Act passed   7.

Questions for Critical Thought

1. How did the new industrial economy after 1871 differ from the previous industrial economy? What
    caused the changes? What effects did they have on society?

2.   Explain and describe the rise of socialism in its various forms after 1870. What caused its diffusion, and what were its attractions?

3.   Outline the class structure that developed in the new urban industrial society. How was it like and unlike earlier structures? What were its strengths and weaknesses?

4.   What were the various roles of women in the new social structure? Did women live better or worse lives than in previous times?

5.   Why and how did urban industrialism lead to more emphasis on education and leisure? How do we still see these effects?

6.   Compare the democracies of Britain and France. How did each nation's history contribute to these developments?

7.   What form did the new German state take? What is Bismarck's role in its formation?

8.   How does Russia's history at the old century's end explain its violent history in the century to come?

Analysis of Primary Source Documents

1.   Explain why department stores proved so successful. What needs did they satisfy, and what sound economic principles did they follow?

2.   What arguments did Edward Bernstein have with the Marxist view of history? To what extent was he still really a Marxist?

3.   Using Octavia Hill as your example, show how early reformers combined compassion for the poor with shrewd business senses.

4.   Give the response one of today's feminists would likely make to Elizabeth Poole Sanford's advice to women. Let your answer be more than one word.

5.   What moral values are reflected by and celebrated in the H.B. Tristam fight song? What kind of men does English public school football want to produce?

6.   According to the account left to us by Louise Michel, what was the purpose of the Paris Commune uprising, and what did it achieve?

7.   To what extent was Bismarck, by trying to eliminate Socialist influence, forced to become a Socialist? How did his motives for social welfare differ from that of the Socialists?

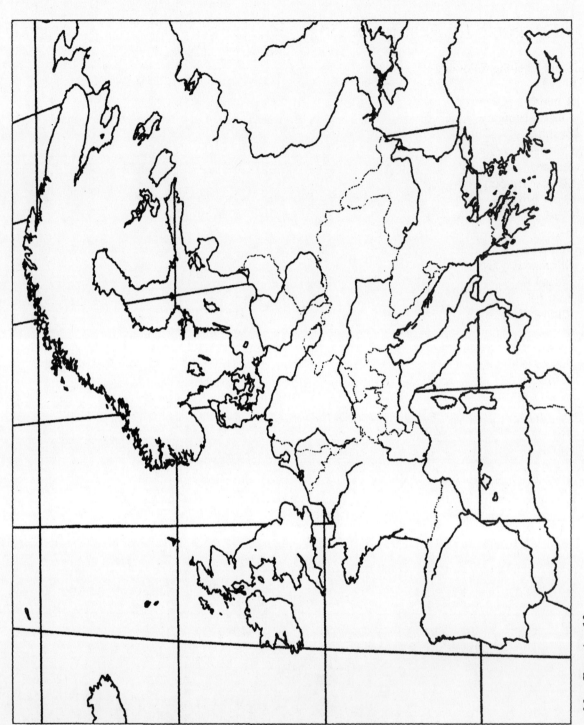

Map Exercise 13

MAP EXERCISE 13: EUROPE IN 1871

Shade and label the following:

1. Algeria
2. Austria-Hungary
3. Bosnia
4. Croatia-Slovenia
5. France
6. German Empire
7. Great Britain
8. Greece
9. Italy
10. Morocco
11. Ottoman Empire
12. Poland
13. Portugal
14. Russian Empire
15. Serbia
16. Spain
17. Switzerland
18. Tunisia

CHAPTER TWENTY-FOUR
AN AGE OF MODERNITY, ANXIETY, AND IMPERIALISM, 1894-1914

Chapter Outline

I.   Toward the Modern Consciousness: Intellectual and Cultural Developments
   A.   Emergence of a New Physics
      1.   Marie Curie and Radium
      2.   Max Planck and Quanta
      3.   Albert Einstein and Relativity
   B.   New Understanding of the Irrational
      1.   Friedrich Nietzsche and Superman
      2.   Henri Bergson and the "Life Force"
      3.   Georges Sorel and Violence
   C.   Sigmund Freud and Psychoanalysis
      1.   Unconscious
      2.   Repression
   D.   Social Darwinism and Racism
      1.   Herbert Spencer's *Social Statistics*
      2.   Friedrich von Bernhardi's Nationalism: *Volk*
   E.   Attack on Christianity and Church Responses
      1.   Ernst Renan's *Life of Jesus*
      2.   Pius IX and Leo XIII
      3.   William Booth and the Salvation Army
   F.   Culture of Modernity
      1.   Literature
         a.   Emile Zola's Naturalism
         b.   Tolstoy and Dostoevsky
         c.   Yeats, Rilke, and Symbolism
      2.   Art
         a.   Pissarro, Monet, Morisot, and Impressionism
         b.   Cezanne, Van Gogh, and Post-Impressionism
         c.   Picasso, Kandinsky, and Abstraction
      3.   Music
         a.   Grieg's Nationalism
         b.   Debussy's Impressionism
         c.   Stravinsky's Primitivism

II.   Politics: New Directions and New Uncertainties
   A.   Women's Rights Movement
      1.   Custody and Property
      2.   Suffrage
      3.   New Woman: Maria Montessori
   B.   Jews in the European Nation-State
      1.   Christian Socialism's Racism
      2.   Theodor Herzl and Zionism

C. Liberalism Transformed
    1. Britain: Liberalism's Failure and the Labor Party
    2. France: Anti-Semitism and Third Republic
D. Growing Tensions in Germany
E. Austria-Hungary: Nationalities
F. Imperial Russia
    1. Industrialization and Socialism
    2. The Revolution of 1905
G. Rise of the United States
H. Growth of Canada

III. New Imperialism
  A. Causes
    1. Competition between European Nations
    2. Social Darwinism and Racism
    3. Humanitarianism and Missions
    4. Economic Gain
  B. Creation of Empires
    1. Scramble for Africa
      a. Cape Colony and the Boer War
      b. Cecil Rhodes and British Strength
      c. Other African Empires
    2. Asia in an Age of Imperialism
      a. James Cook and Australia
      b. China and the "Open Door"
      c. Matthew Perry and Japan
      d. Pacific Islands
  C. Responses to Imperialism
    1. African Colonial Confusion
    2. Boxers and a Chinese Republic
    3. Meiji Modernization of Japan
    4. British Control of India
    5. Results

IV. International Rivalry and the Coming of War
  A. Bismarckian System of Alliances
  B. New Directions and New Crises
    1. Triple Alliance and Triple Entente
    2. Crisis in the Balkans

Chapter Summary

The period from 1894 to 1914 saw Europe expand its horizons, both in the rise of daring, new intellectual and cultural developments at home and in the creation of new empires abroad.

At home scientists worked on theories that in time relegated the old Newtonian world to the past and usher in a much more insecure and dangerous world. Sigmund Freud concluded that man operates at the direction of unconscious motivations. The teachings of Charles Darwin were applied to society and used to justify racism and imperialism by saying that in the struggle of races and nations the fittest survive and make the world a better place. Christianity did constant battle with forces that threatened it. Impressionism and Abstraction appeared in literature, the arts, and music.

The old empires in America and India had long either been lost or integrated into the European system when the Western nations began a second round of modern empire building toward the end of the nineteenth century. In a quarter century almost all of Africa was carved up and portioned out to be colonies of European nations; and in that same period Asia as well was divided into spheres of influence and trade. While the two old established Asian nations remained independent, China and Japan were also deeply affected and changed by Western imperialism. China was opened to trade and to Western concessions, leading to a violent native rebellion and to a revolution that toppled the Manchu Dynasty and established a Chinese republic. Japan opened up to the modern world to the extent that it adopted Western military, educational, governmental, and financial ways, even to the extent of taking colonies of its own in China and Korea.

Amid this ferment and expansionism the clouds of war gathered. The great nations of Europe, competing with and fearing each other, formed defensive alliances with friends against foes and stockpiled weapons for a conflict that seemed to be more inevitable by the certainty of combatants that it could not be avoided.

Learning Objectives

1. Be able to discuss the "intellectual ferment" of the late nineteenth century and the new ideas that competed for attention.

2. Examine the status of European Jews, why the idea of Zionism proved so appealing to many of them, and why it was not implemented.

3. Discuss the important political changes seen in Western Europe and the United States at the turn of the twentieth century.

4. Explain why Europe pursued a new imperialism toward the end of the nineteenth century and how the creation of broad empires proved so relatively easy.

5. Describe the international rivalries and intrigues that made it likely there would be a major war at the beginning of the twentieth century.

Glossary of Names and Terms

1. Relativity: Einstein's theory that time and space are not absolute but are relative to the subjective observer.

2. Superman: the kind of new being that Nietzsche believed could emerge if men threw off the slave mentality imposed on them by Christianity.

3. Repression: the process by which Freud believed people submerge painful memories but do not escape their unconscious effects on their behavior.

4. *Volk*: the Germany concept of their nation or race, implying for many a German racial superiority and right to rule over "lesser" peoples.

5. Leo XIII: pope who responded to the challenges of modern thinking by permitting the theory of evolution to be taught in Catholic schools and commended socialism's humanitarianism.

6. Primitivism: a movement in music to return to less refined and more genuinely human emotions by the use of folk tunes and dances.

7   Zionism: the movement, inspired by continuing anti-Semitism and most dramatically represented by Theodor Herzl, for Jews to establish a nation in Palestine.

8. Rhodesia: African colony named for the British gold and diamond merchant Cecil Rhodes, a leading imperialist.

9. "Open Door": policy agreed to by western powers on how to treat China, a system in which each nation established "concessions" along the China coast.

10. Meiji: the name (Enlightened) given to the rule of Japanese emperor Mutsuhito, during which time Japan made dramatic strides to catch up technologically to the western world.

Match These Words with Their Definitions:

1. Herbert Spencer

2. Ernst Renan

3. Wassily Kandinsky

4. Igor Stravinsky

5. Boers

6. Cecil Rhodes

7. James Cook

8. Manchus

9. Boxers

10. Meiji

A. British captain who first explored Australia

B. Anti-foreign movement in turn-of-the-century China

C. Era when Japan became a modern nation

D. Abstract expressionist who led flight from "visual reality"

E. Descendants of Dutch emigrants to southern Africa

F. Composer of the revolutionary *Rite of Spring*

G. Most prominent exponent of Social Darwinism

H. Diamond merchant who tried to overthrow the government of the South African Republic

I. Wrote of Jesus as a man

J. Last dynastic house of China, overthrown in 1912

Choose the Correct Answer:

1. Max Planck's discovery of "quanta" energy

    a. brought Newtonian physics into serious question.
    b. proved that atoms radiate energy in a steady stream.
    c. reaffirmed the belief that science accurately describes reality.
    d. led to massive demonstrations in Russia.
    e. was quickly surpassed by Einstein's discovery of relativity.

2. Nietzsche's "Superman" would

    a. lead Germany to victory over the French.
    b. eliminate the Christian or "slave" mentality.
    c. reform the Church and restore true Christianity.
    d. teach German children better Christian morals.
    e. entertain the masses with feats of super strength.

3. Albert Einstein

   a. worked with Max Planck to develop the quantum theory.
   b. was from his early career welcomed into the European scientific community.
   c. developed a theory in which neither time nor space exists independent of human experience.
   d. confirmed the Newtonian scheme of the universe as one with absolute time and space.
   e. carefully avoided speaking of his ethnic background.

4. Sigmund Freud believed that the way to solve the conflicts of his patients was to

   a. trace repression back to its childhood origins.
   b. use electrotherapy along with drugs.
   c. help them override the pleasure principle.
   d. bring their superegos under strict control.
   e. teach them to be independent of their parents.

5. Advocates of Social Darwinism in the late nineteenth century called for

   a. more government aid to science education.
   b. socialist welfare programs to help those who are economically weak.
   c. a moratorium on war in order to save mankind from destruction.
   d. national medical care programs for those unable to pay for it themselves.
   e. an international struggle to prove what peoples were fittest to survive.

6. The German concept of the *Volk*

   a. proclaimed that German culture was the world's highest.
   b. led to the belief that the Jews were out to destroy the Aryan race.
   c. represented the direction Social Darwinism took in that country.
   d. all of the above
   e. none of the above

7. The growing challenges to Christian churches from science and modern thought resulted in

   a. harsh criticism of socialism by Pope Leo XIII in his *De Rerum Novarum.*
   b. admission of Catholic shortcomings by Pope Pius IX in his *Syllabus of Errors.*
   c. a portrait of Jesus as a non-divine person by Ernst Renan in his *Life of Jesus.*
   d. the eventual adoption of Modernist thought both by Protestants and Catholics.
   e. severe suppression of scientific inquiry in Germany and Russia.

8. Zola's literary Naturalism was deeply influenced by

   a. Freud's theory of the Unconscious.
   b. Herzl's call for a Jewish state.
   c. Darwin's theory of the struggle for survival.
   d. Nietzsche's call for a Superman.
   e. Marx's prediction of a Communist revolution.

9. Dostoevsky's life experiences led him to believe that

    a. by turning to socialism the world could be saved.
    b. Russia needed a Japanese form of emperor worship.
    c. the Church must revert to poverty in order to be Christ-like.
    d. man's soul is purified through suffering.
    e. repressed memories caused most violent behavior.

10. The early feminist movement was most widely known for

    a. its alliance with the trade union movement.
    b. achievements in nursing by Sieveking and Nightingale.
    c. iconoclastic speeches by the German leader Millicent Fawcett.
    d. achieving woman suffrage across Europe by 1914.
    e. violence against elected officials, especially in France.

11. The first recorded martyr to the cause of women's suffrage was

    a. Millicent Fawcett, starved by prison guards.
    b. Emily Davison, trampled by the king's horse.
    c. Bertha von Suttner, believed poisoned by male colleagues.
    d. Emmeline Pankhurst, drowned by water from fire hoses.
    e. Aletta Jacob, killed in a fire bombing of her birth control clinic.

12. Theodor Herzl's *Jewish State* concluded that

    a. Jews should remain in Europe and wait for the tide of anti-Semitism to turn.
    b. the Zionist movement was a Utopian dream that should best be abandoned.
    c. the creation of a Jewish nation in Palestine was both feasible and advisable.
    d. a separate Jewish homeland would never be tolerated by the European nations.
    e. Jews are the super race, as proven by their accomplishments in science and the arts.

13. Europeans justified their nineteenth century imperialism as

    a. necessary to maintain national and international prestige.
    b. a moral responsibility of Europeans to bring civilization to other peoples.
    c. part of the natural order as outlined by the Social Darwinists.
    d. all of the above
    e. none of the above

14. European imperialism in Africa was best characterized by

    a. grossly mismatched battles in which Europeans easily defeated native resistance.
    b. the battle for North Africa between the Germans and the Turks.
    c. rivalries between European powers leading to full-scale wars on the African continent.
    d. cooperative and equitable agreements between Europeans and native Africans.
    e. Europe's willingness to permit American colonies on the west coast.

15. The Englishman Cecil Rhodes carved out an African colony of his own by

    a.   converting natives of the Transvaal to Christianity.
    b.   monopolizing the sale of precious commodities.
    c.   leading an army composed of native and Indian mercenaries to victory.
    d.   persuading the Boers to name him their prime minister.
    e.   promising to educate natives for civil service jobs in the British Empire.

16. Which of the following statements best applies to European imperialism in Asia?

    a.   Russia showed little interest in Asia until 1918.
    b.   The British acquired the Philippines in a war with Spain.
    c.   China was divided by the great powers into spheres of influence.
    d.   The United States dominated Southeast Asia after 1895.
    e.   Japan was considered too poor for colonial exploitation.

17. Choose the correct relationship between the Asian nation and its response to European imperialism.

    a.   China—the educated classes entered British civil service, but they continued to be resentful of
         the foreign devils.
    b.   India—anti-foreign violence in the Boxer Rebellion resulted in the British imposing harsher
         colonial rule.
    c.   Japan—rapidly adopted Western military and industrial techniques in order to become an
         imperial power itself.
    d.   Philippines—won independence from the Americans through a series of daring and destructive
         raids on U.S. military bases.
    e.   Siam—used a British school mistress to persuade Dutch authorities from making Bangkok a
         protectorate.

18. Meiji Japan imitated

    a.   the U.S. in military and Germany in industrial matters.
    b.   France in military and Britain in industrial matters.
    c.   Britain in military and France in industrial matters.
    d.   Germany in military and the U.S. in industrial matters.
    e.   Germany in industrial and the U.S. in military matters.

19. Nineteenth-century British India saw

    a.   many educated Indians achieving high positions in the civil service.
    b.   an organized independence movement which threatened British rule.
    c.   the devastation of the countryside due to a series of internal wars.
    d.   progress in the production and distribution of food.
    e.   few changes in the lives of natives, who remained illiterate and malnourished.

20. Following the dismissal of Bismarck by William II in 1890, Germany

    a.   Became increasingly active in foreign affairs, pursuing its "place in the sun"
    b.   Became ever more closely allied with Britain
    c.   Abandoned plans for building a navy and concentrated fully on building its army
    d.   Succeeded in splitting the Entente Cordiale agreed to by Britain and France
    e.   Adopted a policy of avoiding military conflict "at all costs"

Complete the Following Sentences:

1. Max Planck concluded that bodies radiate energy in irregular packets called _____, thus creating questions about the old view of _____ and the physics of _____ _____.

2. Einstein's special theory of _____ said space and time are not absolute but depend upon the _____, and he elaborated that if matter disappeared, so too would _____ and _____.

3. Freud taught that human behavior is largely affected by the _____, a body of former experiences of which we are _____, but which often appear in coded form in _____.

4. Friedrich von Bernhardi added to the theory of Social _____ the claim that _____, which he considered a _____ necessity, is "the father of all things."

5. Pope Leo XIII upheld the right of private _____ yet criticized "naked" _____; and he called much that was in _____ Christian, while condemning _____ for being materialistic and anti-religious.

6. Pissarro and Monet painted nature directly, seeking to capture the first _____ and to show the changing effects of _____ on nature, thus laying the foundations for _____ painting.

7. In the late nineteenth century European nations came to dominate _____ and _____, two areas largely ignored earlier. Despite claims that they acted for _____ reasons, this was in fact a "new _____."

8. The Boers made their Great Trek and set up governments in the _____ and the _____ _____ _____ in order to escape being ruled by the _____.

9. Although the Society of Harmonious Fists, known to Europeans as _____, tried to free China from foreign control, other Chinese revolutionaries, led by Dr. _____ _____ _____, worked to overthrow the _____ dynasty.

10. Emperor Mutsuhito of Japan, calling his reign the _____, sought to transform his society by reform and conquest, claiming territory on the _____ mainland and annexing _____ after defeating _____ in 1905.

Place the Following in Chronological Order and Give Dates:

1. Boxer Rebellion in China   1.

2. Three Emperors' League formed   2.

3. British take Hong Kong   3.

4. Japan annexes Korea   4.

5. Victoria crowned Empress of India   5.

6. Suez Canal opened   6.

7. Triple Entente formed   7.

Questions for Critical Thought

1. What new ideas were introduced into the world of science—particularly physics and psychology—near the turn of the twentieth century? Why did such ideas so often meet with "irrational" responses from philosophers?

2. How did Freud's analysis of human nature depart from previous analyses? To what extent did Freudian analysis become "the future" of anthropology?

3. Explain Social Darwinism, and show how it helped give direction and legitimacy to a new wave of racism. What were Jewish responses to the related phenomenon of anti-Semitism?

4. Describe turn-of-the-century "attacks" on organized Christianity, and show how the churches responded to what they saw as threats.

5. Discuss the various forms that turn-of-the-century art, architecture, and literature took. Give an overall explanation for these movements. Where did the arts seem headed in 1914?

6. How and why did the feminist movement come about? In what ways was it a product of its times?

7. Describe the "new imperialism" of the late nineteenth century. How was it different from the earlier European imperialism? What were its causes and results? How did Europe's Asia and African empires differ?

8. Describe the system of alliances that both held off war until 1914 and then helped bring it on. What brought the long European peace to an end?

Analysis of Primary Source Documents

1. What do you learn of Freud's methodology by reading his lecture on repression? What explanation do you find here for the immense prestige he gained in his own lifetime?

2. Read aloud, then describe the "feeling" Rimbaud's poem gives you. In what sense does he give "meaning without meaning" to a reader?

3. How would a typical woman of 1879 have felt watching a performance of Ibsen's *A Doll's House*? What might "Nora" have said to women had she turned and addressed the audience directly?

4. What parts of Theodor Herzl's proposal for a Jewish homeland came true, and what parts did not? How different is today's nation of Israel from Herzl's dream?

5. Explain how the events of "Bloody Sunday" fit into the Russian year 1905. What does the firing upon the crowd say about the tsar's government at that time?

6. What was Kipling's "white man's burden," how were white men to bear it, and what would be their reward?

7. Using Morel's *Black Man's Burden*, explain the damage colonialism did to African people, their society, and their culture.

8. In his 1908 interview with the British *Daily Telegraph*, Kaiser William II spoke his mind. What did he mean to say, and how did he end up saying it? How do you account for the difference?

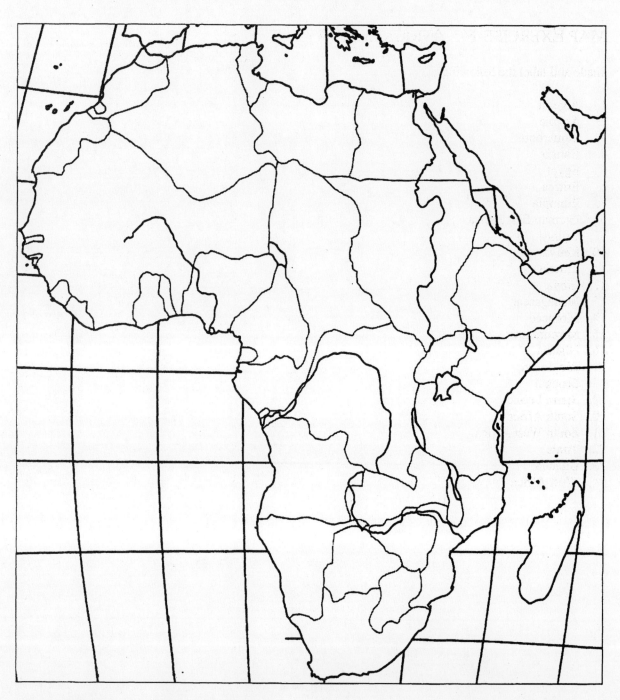

Map Exercise 14

MAP EXERCISE 14: AFRICA IN 1914

Shade and label the following:

1. Algeria
2. Angola
3. Cameroon
4. Congo
5. Egypt
6. Eritrea
7. Ethiopia
8. German East Africa
9. Guinea
10. Kenya
11. Liberia
12. Libya
13. Madagascar
14. Morocco
15. Mozambique
16. Nigeria
17. Rio de Oro
18. Senegal
19. Sierra Leone
20. South Africa
21. South West Africa
22. Tunis
23. Uganda
24. West Africa

CHAPTER TWENTY-FIVE

THE BEGINNING OF THE TWENTIETH-CENTURY CRISIS: WAR AND REVOLUTION

Chapter Outline

I. Road to World War I
    A. Nationalism and Internal Dissent
        1. Growing National Rivalries
        2. Diplomacy on the Constant Brink of War
        3. Dissatisfaction of Ethnic Minorities
    B. Militarism
        1. Large Armies
        2. Contingency Plans for War
    C. Outbreak of War: Summer of 1914
        1. Austria's Troubles in the Balkans
        2. Assassination of Francis Ferdinand
        3. Alliances Bring General War
        4. Germany's Schlieffen Plan

II. The War
    A. 1914-1915: Illusions and Stalemate
        1. Enthusiasm and Expectations for a Brief War
        2. French Defensive
        3. German Successes in the East
    B. 1916-1017: Great Slaughter
        1. Trench Warfare
        2. Hardships of the Average Soldier
    C. Widening of the War
        1. Balkans and Gallipoli
        2. Global Conflict
        3. Entry of the United States
    D. New Kind of Warfare
    E. Home Front: Impact of Total War
        1. Political Centralization and Economic Regimentation
        2. Public Order and Public Opinion
            a. Irish Uprising
            b. Army Mutinies
        3. Social Impact of Total War
            a. Benefits to Labor
            b. New Roles for Women
            c. Challenges to Class
            d. Inflation

III. War and Revolution
    A. Russian Revolution
        1. March Revolution and a Provisional Government
        2. Lenin and the Bolshevik (October) Revolution

       3. Treaty of Brest-Litovsk
       4. Civil War
  B. Last Year of the War: 1918
       1. Germany's Last Gamble
       2. Armistice: November 11
       3. War Casualties
  C. Revolutions in Germany and Austria
       1. New German Republic
       2. Division of the Austrian Empire

IV. Paris Peace Settlement
  A. Big Four
       1. Wilson's Ideals: The Fourteen Points
       2. Quest for Reward and Retribution
  B. Treaty of Versailles
       1. Dismemberment of Empires
       2. Failure of Vision
       3. League of Nations
       4. America's New Isolationism
       5. End of European Hegemony

Chapter Summary

The twentieth century really began not in 1900 but with the outbreak of World War I in 1914. The Great War, as it was called until a second world war broke out in 1939, ended the military alliances and styles of the life left over from the century past and ushered in the new world of a truly new century.

In the summer of 1914, Archduke Francis Ferdinand of Austria-Hungary was assassinated in the Bosnian capital of Sarajevo, and within six weeks the major nations of Europe were at war with each other in accordance with their myriad treaties, many of them until that time kept secret. For over a quarter of a century the growth of nationalistic competition had combined with an equally dangerous growth in military weaponry all across the continent to make Europe a powder keg waiting to burst into flame. The assassination was but the spark that brought ignition.

Since Germany had no trouble defeating Russian armies, it became evident quite early in the conflict that the war would be won and lost on the Western Front, between Germany and the Allies, Britain and France. Yet the war dragged on for four long years, much of it fought from trenches, as morale dropped lower and lower. Unrest spread through both camps and at home, where the belligerents had to keep their civilian populations in line with unusually harsh measures. Only in Russia did the government lose control; and there the tsar and his family were murdered, ushering in a new regime. Out of the chaos that followed the March Revolution, Lenin's Bolshevik Party finally emerged triumphant. Russia was then a Communist state for over seventy years.

When the war eventually ended, the two losers experienced the revolutions that had threatened them during the war; and both Germany and Austria became republics. The victors met in Paris to make the peace and themselves could not agree on whether to establish a new and just world order or punish the Germans. Eventually they created an order that virtually assured that there would be another world war in the future.

Learning Objectives

1. Be able to outline the conditions that made World War I probable and to explain why and how it began as it did.
2. Trace the most important turning points in the shifting fortunes of the various nations involved in the war.

3. Describe the effects total war had on the home fronts of the nations engaged on the battlefields.

4. Discuss and account for the differing attitudes and goals of the Big Four at Versailles, and show how the differences led to failure.

5. Analyze the peace treaties that ended the war, and show how they gave the world little hope that more wars could be avoided.

Glossary of Names and Terms

1. Black Hand: Serbian organization dedicated to the creation of a pan-Slavic kingdom, members of which assassinated the Austrian archduke in 1914.

2. Gallipoli: site of a failed attempt by British forces to open a front against the Central Powers in the Balkans.

3. Easter Rebellion: uprising on Easter Sunday 1916 in Dublin in an Irish nationalist attempt to overthrow British rule.

4. DORA: British Defense of the Realm Act, which permitted the government to censor newspapers and arrest dissenters as traitors.

5. Hemophilia: a disease that prevents the clotting of blood, suffered by the heir to the Russian throne, placing the empire in peril.

6. Bolsheviks: the majority party within the Russian Communist movement, led by Lenin, the group that came to power in October, 1917.

7. Brest-Litovsk: site where the Russian Communist government made peace with Germany, ending the war on the eastern front.

8. Rosa Luxemburg: German Communist Party leader, who led a movement to take control of the government at the end of the war and was brutally murdered by the army.

9. The Fourteen Points: U.S. President Woodrow Wilson's plan for settlement of World War I, the only one of which became reality was the League of Nations.

10. War Guilt Clause: the part of the Peace of Paris that blamed Germany for starting World War I, an admission it was required to make, one that caused great resentment.

Match These Words with Their Definitions:

1.	Alfred von Schlieffen	A.	Gave permission for Britain to arrest war dissenters as traitors
2.	Paul von Hindenburg	B.	Lenin's plan of the Bolshevik revolution
3.	Lusitania	C.	Bolshevik secret police
4.	DORA	D.	Commander of first victories in World War I
5.	Rasputin	E.	Site of Russian-German peace conference
6.	April Theses	F.	Leader of effort to blame and punish Germany for the war
7.	Brest-Litovsk	G.	British ship sunk in 1915 with the loss of 100 American lives
8.	Cheka	H.	Socialist leader of the new German republic of 1918
9.	Friedrich Ebert	I.	"Holy man" assassinated in 1916
10.	Georges Clemenceau	J.	Author of the first German plan of attack

Choose the Correct Answer:

1. Before the outbreak of World War I in 1914, most Europeans were

    a. highly optimistic about the future, expecting material progress to continue to the establishment of an "earthly paradise."
    b. extremely indifference about the future and recklessness in their pursuit of physical pleasures.
    c. extremely pessimistic, believing war to be inevitable and the end of the world probably close at hand.
    d. completely dependent on the good graces of socialistic governments and slovenly in their work habits.
    e. looking to the United States to prevent or settle future wars.

2. The rivalry between which two states for domination of southeastern Europe helped create serious tensions just before World War I?

    a. Germany and Italy
    b. Russia and Italy
    c. Austria-Hungary and Russia
    d. Britain and France
    e. Russia and the Ottoman Empire

3. The immediate cause of the start of World War I was

    a. French fears of a growing German military.
    b. the assassination of Archduke Francis Ferdinand.
    c. the German invasion of Poland.
    d. British refusal to permit German to expand its navy.
    e. revelations about a new German weapon, the u-boat.

4. In August, 1914, most of the participants believed that the war was

   a.   the opening act of an international communist revolution.
   b.   being fought to defend their countries from aggression.
   c.   a way to determine which nations were fittest to survive.
   d.   a good way to revive Europe's flagging economy.
   e.   punishment for Europe's recent immorality.

5. The most important characteristic of the first year of World War I was

   a.   stalemate on the Western Front after the First Battle of the Marne.
   b.   Italy's fateful decision to switch over to the German and Austrian side.
   c.   the weakness of the German army on the Russian Front.
   d.   Serbia's success in winning independence from the Austrian Empire.
   e.   the outbreak of the Russian Revolution.

6. Trench warfare on the Western Front was characterized by

   a.   quick advances and seizures of land back and forth.
   b.   few casualties because of good fortifications and lack of engagement.
   c.   dreary boredom and static routines accompanied by increasing illness.
   d.   high morale and assurance of imminent victory by both sides.
   e.   feverish attempts by leaders on both sides to break the stalemate.

7. The British officer T. E. Lawrence

   a.   spent the war years as an undercover spy in Germany.
   b.   perfected the motorcycle for use in desert warfare.
   c.   signed the armistice agreement November 11, 1918.
   d.   incited Arab princes to rebel against the Turks.
   e.   was found guilty of treason under the Defense of the Realm Act.

8. The United States finally decided to enter the war because of

   a.   the sinking of the Lusitania.
   b.   Germany's refusal to stop unrestricted submarine warfare.
   c.   President Wilson's dream of ending war forever.
   d.   the assassination of the American ambassador in Vienna.
   e.   Germany's attempt to get Mexico to invade the United States.

9. The entry of the United States into World War I

   a.   gave the Allies a much needed psychological boost.
   b.   made the German Naval Staff contemplate surrender.
   c.   was in response to Turkey's entrance on the side of Germany.
   d.   put an end to Germany's use of submarine warfare.
   e.   immediately made America the arbiter of the peace.

10. Irish attitudes toward the war were demonstrated by

    a.   the number of Irish who worked in English factories.
    b.   an uprising against British rule on Easter Sunday.
    c.   an official declaration of support for the Allies.
    d.   the "Irish Brigade" which fought at the Second Battle of the Marne.
    e.   an Irish attempt to assassinate David Lloyd George.

11. As public morale weakened in the later stages of the war

    a.   governments brutally and successfully suppressed all labor strikes.
    b.   Clemenceau's liberal French government bowed to popular demands.
    c.   most governments stopped printing propaganda, considering it a waste of time.
    d.   many pastors and priests identified patriotism as a Christian duty.
    e.   police were given the power to charge dissenters as traitors.

12. Women hired for wartime work generally believed their jobs were

    a.   critical to the war effort.
    b.   tasks men could do much better if they were available.
    c.   temporary and would end with the war.
    d.   patriotic obligations, fully as important as battle.
    e.   poor compensation for not being allowed to fight in battle.

13. The most obvious gain for women due to their work during the war was

    a.   an increase in their numbers of women at universities in the democracies.
    b.   a new attitude toward divorce and abortion in France and England.
    c.   the right to vote granted in Britain, Austria, and Germany.
    d.   the granting of full pensions to all wartime nurses.
    e.   acceptance into postwar military academies.

14. The most visible effect of World War I on British society was a

    a.   lessening and decline of class distinctions.
    b.   lessening of chronic criminal behavior.
    c.   dramatic increase in church membership and attendance.
    d.   new optimistic, positive outlook on the part of young people.
    e.   determination henceforth to follow a policy of preemptive war.

15. Which of the following best describes wartime Russia?

    a.   Prime minister Rasputin proved a careful domestic manager.
    b.   The Tsarina Alexandra kept Nicholas ignorant of domestic problems.
    c.   The general population, despite hardships, was supportive throughout the war.
    d.   Numerous social and economic reforms kept the peasants happy.
    e.   The general public knew little about severe losses on the battlefield.

16. Lenin returned to Russia in 1917

    a.   in order to urge Socialists to support the war effort.
    b.   despite German attempts to keep him in France.
    c.   on a French ship with forged British documents.
    d.   from exile in Switzerland with German aid.
    e.   only to be exiled to Siberia until the next year.

17. Which of the following statements best applies to Lenin?

    a.   He accepted a central figure in the Provisional Government.
    b.   In his "April Theses" he renounced violence and advocated evolutionary socialism.
    c.   His middle-class background kept him from being as radical as Trotsky.
    d.   He promised that the Bolsheviks would redistribute all Russian lands to the peasants.
    e.   A heart condition limited his activities to writing and making speeches.

18. The Second Battle of the Marne was

    a.   Germany's final desperate effort to win the war.
    b.   proof that Hindenburg had lost control of military policy.
    c.   irrelevant to the outcome of the war.
    d.   all of the above
    e.   none of the above

19. At the end of the war, Woodrow Wilson wanted most of all to

    a.   punish Germany for its war crimes.
    b.   assure self-determination for all peoples.
    c.   strengthen America's influence in Europe.
    d.   bring down the Soviet Union.
    e.   eliminate all military forces from the continent of Europe.

20. At the Paris Peace Conference, Clemenceau of France wanted

    a.   Germany to be demilitarized.
    b.   Germany to pay for the costs of the war.
    c.   a separate Rhineland as a buffer between Germany and France.
    d.   all three of the above
    e.   none of the first three

Complete the Following Sentences:

1. Among the ethnic minorities hoping in 1914 for nationhood were the _____ in Britain, the _____ in Russia, and the _____ in Austria-Hungary.

2. Archduke Francis Ferdinand's assassin was a _____ who worked for a _____ terrorist organization called the _____ _____.

3. A French counterattack under General _____ in 1914 stopped the German army at the _____ River and led to a long period of _____ warfare.

4. The great slaughters of World War I's Western Front occurred in the German offensive at _____, the British campaign on the _____, and the French attack in the _____.

5. A British war humor magazine said there were two kinds of DUDS: one a _____ that fails to explode; two an official who draws a big _____ and _____ for no reason.

6. The United States was at last drawn into World War I in April, 1917, by the German decision to use unrestricted _____ _____. This gave the Allies more a _____ than a military boost.

7. When General _____ and his deputy _____ took control of the German government in 1916, they mobilized for _____ _____.

8. David Lloyd George, who became the British _____ _____ in 1916, believed that the war would eliminate domestic _____ conflict in Britain.

9. The 1917 March Revolution in Russia established a _____ Government, but it was overthrown within a year by the _____ led by _____.

10. American president Woodrow Wilson came to Paris with an idealistic plan for peace, his _____ _____: but he met resistance from leaders of _____ and _____, both of whom wanted first and foremost to punish Germany.

Place the Following in Chronological Order and Give Dates:

1. Treaty of Brest-Litovsk signed   1.

2. Armistice between Allies and Germany   2.

3. Second Battle of the Marne   3.

4. Paris Conference begins   4.

5. Archduke Francis Ferdinand assassinated   5.

6. Beginning of World War I   6.

7. The United States enters the war   7.

Questions for Critical Thought

1. What were the conditions, factors, and events that led—both directly and indirectly—to the outbreak of World War I?

2. Chart the development of the Great War in its two-year periods. Explain why it went on for so long and what finally hastened its end.

3. What impact did this "total war" have on life at home? How were domestic, economic, and political moments affected by it?

4.   How did World War I lead to the revolution in Russia? How did it affect that final outcome of that internal struggle?

5.   Recount the story of the Russian Revolution, from the abdication of the Tsar, until the end of the ensuing civil war. How do these events help explain Russia today?

6.   Why was the United States so late getting into the war? What role did the U.S. play in it once it was involved?

7.   How did the national revolutions in Austria and Germany differ from the one in Russia? What accounts for the differences? What long-term consequences did they have for European affairs?

8.   Describe the Paris Peace Conference and the Treaty of Versailles. Why were they later deemed failures? To what extent did they assure another world war?

9.   How did its involvement in World War I change the role of the United States in world affairs? In spite of its attempt, after the war, to return to isolationism, why was this not in the end possible?

Analysis of Primary Source Documents

1.   Describe how and why the emperors of Germany and Russia interpreted the events of July 1914 so differently. What possible compromises were still open at that time, and why did these men not attempt them?

2.   Describe and explain the exhilaration people felt upon entering the Great War. What lessons were they about to learn? What lessons can their naivete teach us today?

3.   How would you know, had you not been told, that Remarque himself experienced trench warfare? Explain why his account of it is so powerful.

4.   Compare and contrast the songs sung about the Great War by Germans, British, and Americans. What historical experiences and national characteristics are evident in the words?

5.   What did Naomi Loughnan learn in her munitions factory about working-class men and women? What were various classes and genders learning from each other there?

6.   What do his brief letters tell you about John Mott? What is the reason for and meaning of his constant understatement?

7.   From John Reed's account, what do you think made Lenin the leader of the Russian Revolution? What does Reed mean by Lenin's "intellect"?

8.   How did Woodrow Wilson and Georges Clemenceau differ in their assessments of the war? Why did Clemenceau consider Wilson naive and Wilson consider Clemenceau a vindictive bigot?

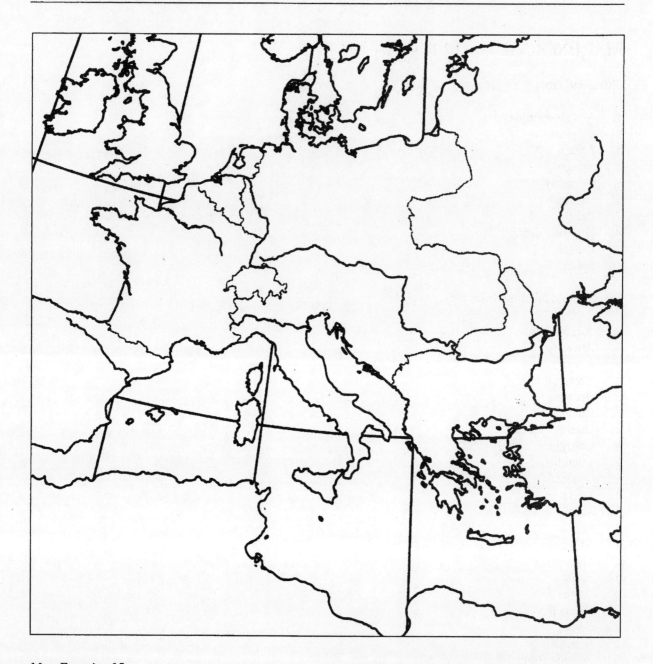

Map Exercise 15

MAP EXERCISE 15: EUROPE IN 1914

Shade and label the following:

1. Austria-Hungary
2. Belgium
3. Britain
4. France
5. Germany
6. Greece
7. Italy
8. Ottoman Empire
9. Russia
10. Spain

Pinpoint and label the following:

1. Amiens
2. Antwerp
3. Berlin
4. Brest-Litovsk
5. Brussels
6. Calais
7. Chateau Thierry
8. Cologne
9. Frankfurt
10. Gallipoli
11. LeHavre
12. Marne River
13. Mons
14. Moscow
15. Oise River
16. Paris
17. Reims
18. Rhine River
19. Sedan
20. Seine River
21. Somme River
22. Vienna

CHAPTER TWENTY-SIX
THE FUTILE SEARCH FOR A NEW STABILITY:
EUROPE BETWEEN THE WARS, 1919-1939

Chapter Outline

I. Uncertain Peace: Search for Security
    A. French Policy of Coercion (1919-1924)
        1. Reparations and Occupation
        2. Economic Crisis and Conciliation
    B. Hopeful Years (1924-1929)
        1. Economic Stability
        2. Germany in the League of Nations
        3. Plan for World Disarmament
    C. Great Depression
        1. American Funds Withdrawn
        2. Stock Market Crash
        3. Governmental Inaction

II. Democratic States
    A. Great Britain
        1. Stanley Baldwin's Conservative Era of Prosperity
        2. National·Government Coalition
    B. France
        1. National Bloc and Cartel of the Left
        2. Leon Blum's Popular Front
    C. Scandinavian Social Democracy
    D. United States and Roosevelt's New Deal
        1. Government Involvement
        2. Persistence of Unemployment
    E. European States and the World: Colonial Empires
        1. Middle East
        2. India
        3. Independence Movements in Africa

III. Retreat from Democracy: Authoritarian and Totalitarian States
    A. Fascist Italy
        1. Anger in Post-war Italy
        2. Benito Mussolini and the Fascist Party
        3. March on Rome
        4. Mussolini and the Fascist State
            a. Limits on Liberties
            b. Single-minded Society
            c. Fascist View of Women
    B. Nazi Germany
        1. Failure of the Weimar Republic
        2. Emergence of Adolf Hitler

   3. National Socialism
      a. Anti-communism and the Reichstag Fire
      b. Totalitarian Rule: Nazi State (1933-1939)
      c. Aryanism and *Kristallnacht*
   C. Soviet Union
      1. Lenin's New Economic Policy
      2. Stalinist Era
         a. State Industrialization
         b. Agricultural Collectivization
         c. Purges
   D. Authoritarianism in Eastern Europe
      1. Military Dictatorship in Poland
      2. Czechoslovakia Alone as a Democracy
   E. Dictatorship in the Iberian Peninsula
      1. Spanish Civil War and Franco
      2. Salazar's Military Portugal

IV. Expansion of Mass Culture and Mass Leisure
   A. Radio and Movies
   B. Travel and Recreation

V. Cultural and Intellectual Trends
   A. Oswald Spengler's Pessimism
   B. Nightmares and New Visions
      1. Dadaism and Surrealism in Art
      2. Functionalism in Architecture
      3. Socialist Realism
      4. Schonberg and Atonal Music
   C. Search for the Unconscious
      1. James Joyce, Virginia Woolf, and Hermann Hesse
      2. Jungian Psychology
   D. Heroic Age of Physics
      1. Ernest Rutherford and the Atom
      2. Werner Heisenberg's Uncertainty Principle

Chapter Summary

   Perceptive observers knew by 1919 that the peace treaty that ended World War I was flawed and insecure. The French, who felt vulnerable to another invasion and abandoned by their former allies, sought to weaken Germany and punish her for past offenses, leading to further hostilities on both sides. There were a few hopeful years, during the late 1920s, with the return of material prosperity; but then the Great Depression of 1929 brought Europe back to the brink of ruin: economic, social, and political.
   The democracies, Britain, France, the Scandinavian countries, and the United States, spent most of the 1930s trying to recover from the crash of 1929, while Eastern and Southern European nations turned even more to authoritarian and totalitarian governments. Following the lead of Fascist Italy, Germany surrendered to Nazi rule. Communism in Russia took a turn to the right under Stalin's iron fist. While Fascism and Communism espoused widely varied philosophies of economics and government, they showed striking similarities in their attitudes toward Democracy. Government of the people, by the people, and for the people appeared to be passing away.
   Popular culture reflected the deepening pessimism of the 1930s. Entertainment was more accessible than ever before, through rapid increases in the numbers of movie theaters and radios; and there was more

time and opportunity for leisure activities than ever; but people seemed driven to pleasure as if it might soon end. Totalitarian regimes used film, radio, and leisure programs to increase their power. The arts, literature, and music reflected the pessimism and irrationality of the day; and physics continued to develop methods that might just as well destroy as save the world. Thunderclouds were gathering.

Learning Objectives

1. Be able to explain why Europe experienced a great depression in the 1930s and how it affected both domestic politics in the democracies and international affairs.

2. Give the common characteristics of the various totalitarian states that emerged between the two world wars.

3. Trace Adolf Hitler's rise to power, what methods he used, what conditions made it possible for him to become Germany's leader, and how his career affected world history.

4. Describe the kind of mass entertainment that attracted people between the wars and how it was used by some governments to control them.

5. Discuss the intellectual and cultural trends of the time between the wars, and explain both what inspired them and their influence on society.

Glossary of Names and Terms

1. Spirit of Locarno: the spirit of hope and cooperation that spread throughout the continent as a result of the international treaty signed there in 1925.

2. John Maynard Keynes: British economist who made concrete proposals on how to survive and overcome the Great Depression.

3. Mohandas Gandhi: Indian leader who began his country's movement for independence in the time between the wars.

4. Fascism: political and social ideology, exemplified by Mussolini and Hitler, which emphasized totalitarian rule and strong nationalism.

5. Beer Hall *Putsch*: the Nazi Party's first attempt to take power, an uprising in Bavaria which led to Hitler's arrest and imprisonment.

6. *Mein Kampf*: the autobiography in which Hitler outlined his political doctrines and goals for the German state he hoped to run.

7. *Hitler Jugend*: organization that trained young German men to follow Hitler without question and be willing to die for the Third Reich.

8. Francisco Franco: army officer who led the successful revolution against the socialist government in Spain and became its fascist dictator for four decades.

9. Arnold Schönberg: composer who invented atonal music, using a scale of twelve tones independent of key.

10. James Joyce: Irish writer whose book *Ulysses* illustrated the technique known as "stream of consciousness," an introduction of interior monologue into the novel.

Match These Words with Their Definitions:

1. Locarno

2. Stanley Baldwin

3. Leon Blum

4. March on Rome

5. Lateran Accords

6. *Lebensraum*

7. Franz von Papen

8. Oswald Spengler

9. Salvador Dali

10. Carl Jung

A. Fascist resolution of Italy's religious question

B. Prime minister for the Popular Front coalition

C. Nazi explanation for eastern expansionism

D. Believed a decadent West was ready to fall

E. Pioneer in the Surrealist school of modern art

F. Spokesman for the "collective unconscious"

G. Where Germany's western borders were guaranteed

H. Arranged for Hitler to come to power in Germany

I. Conservative leader during the prosperous 1920s

J. Action that brought Mussolini to power in Italy

Choose the Correct Answer:

1. Efforts to maintain peace following World War I included

   a. a three-power alliance of Britain, France, and Germany.
   b. the establishment of a peace-keeping League of Nations Army.
   c. a weak alliance between France, Poland, and the Little Entente.
   d. increasing U.S. intervention in European affairs.
   e. a number of successful treaties limiting military growth.

2. The period 1924-1929 in Europe saw

   a. a growing optimism that liberal governments would be able to provide peace and prosperity.
   b. the Great Depression grow worse and eventually swallow up all of Europe.
   c. a continued occupation of Germany by France and Britain.
   d. Western nations cut off all ties with Russia.
   e. democracy hanging on by a thread in Germany and Italy.

3. A major cause of the Great Depression was

   a. European withdrawal from Asian markets.
   b. the recall of American investments from German industries.
   c. rising prices of agricultural products from Eastern Europe.
   d. the Keynesian *laissez-faire* philosophy of economics.
   e. the fall of Italy to the fascists.

4. Economist John Maynard Keynes suggested that the way to overcome the Great Depression might be

    a. a purposeful system of planned unemployment.
    b. a program of strict financial austerity to toughen the economy.
    c. deficit spending and government public works programs.
    d. wholesale government loans to viable businesses.
    e. the establishment of more overseas colonies.

5. One overall effect of the Great Depression in Europe was

    a. the fall of several Communist governments.
    b. high unemployment everywhere but in Great Britain.
    c. a strengthening of liberal democracies.
    d. a noticeable return to traditional religious values.
    e. the rise of fascist movements and governments.

6. The first Popular Front government of France

    a. solved the Depression by eliminating worker benefits.
    b. was led by Socialist Leon Blum, who instituted a French "New Deal."
    c. was led by Fascist Jacques Boulanger, who reoccupied the Ruhr Valley.
    d. collapsed in 1926, when the Leftist Cartel took power.
    e. won the largest popular vote in French history.

7. King Victor Emmanuel III made Mussolini prime minister because

    a. otherwise he would have gone into retirement.
    b. the fascist party won the popular referendum of 1924.
    c. his threat to march on Rome made the democratic government capitulate to him.
    d. there were no other legitimate contenders for the position.
    e. he felt Mussolini could best explain Italy's policies to the other democracies.

8. Which of the following statements best describes Mussolini's Italian Fascist state?

    a. The only element of society the fascists never completely controlled was the press.
    b. Fascist propaganda, laws, and practices forced women to leave the work force and stay at home as wives and mothers.
    c. Giuseppe Bottai's radical education policies enabled the state to create thousands of "new Fascist men."
    d. All religious groups, including Catholics, were portrayed as threats to the unity of the state.
    e. Italian ambassadors were instructed to keep the peace, regardless of the policies of the countries where they served.

9. Mussolini's Fascist dictatorship

    a. lacked an effective secret police force.
    b. included highly popular, well attended youth meetings.
    c. was primarily aimed at aiding workers and peasants.
    d. never achieved the degree of totalitarianism found in Germany and Russia.
    e. was in constant conflict with the papacy.

10. The Lateran Accords of 1929

     a.   nationalized all church property except Vatican City.
     b.   recognized Catholicism as the sole religion of Italy.
     c.   coincided with the Catholic Church's official condemnation of Fascism.
     d.   eliminated all government support for the Catholic Church.
     e.   assured Mussolini that he would have a voice in selection of the next pope.

11. From the writings of Adolf Lanz, a former monk, Hitler got his

     a.   idea of a planned economy to benefit the working class.
     b.   habit of attending Catholic church services each day.
     c.   belief in the superiority of the Aryan race.
     d.   devotion to the principles of vegetarianism.
     e.   plan for the enslavement of the Polish people.

12. On *Kristallnacht*, the German Nazis

     a.   attacked Jewish synagogues and businesses.
     b.   officially welcomed Protestant and Catholic leaders into the party.
     c.   celebrated their first electoral majority victory.
     d.   met to regroup after their first electoral defeat.
     e.   presented Hindenburg with the last of his presidential medals.

13. Heinrich Himmler was responsible for

     a.   forming organizations for professions such as doctors and teachers, to serve the state.
     b.   carrying out SS operations of social and racial terrorism.
     c.   chairing the German Labor Front.
     d.   organizing and directing the *Hitler Jugend*.
     e.   coordinating the program which he named *Kraft durch Freude.*

14. Stalin made his way to power in the Soviet Union as

     a.   Secretary of the Communist Party, making appointments.
     b.   Commissioner of Labor, building the Moscow subway.
     c.   Defense Minister, successfully defeating the Poles.
     d.   Director of the Corps of Engineers, building dams.
     e.   Foreign Minister, making alliances with other Communist governments.

15. The Spanish Civil War ended with the victory of

     a.   King Alfonso XIII and his General Primo de Rivera.
     b.   an antifascist coalition, supported by Soviet troops.
     c.   the conservative National Front, supported by Italy and Germany.
     d.   General Francisco Franco, who established an authoritarian regime.
     e.   the *guarda civil*, supported by the French.

16. *Dopolavoro* and *Kraft durch Freude* were programs designed by fascist governments to

    a. encourage families to produce more children.
    b. increase military awareness and preparedness.
    c. expand production in factories.
    d. provide civilian recreation and mold public opinion.
    e. make agriculture more productive and varied.

17. *Strength through Joy* was

    a. a Nazi propaganda film produced by Joseph Goebbels.
    b. the national recreation program of Fascist Italy.
    c. an attempt to monitor and homogenize the leisure activities of German workers.
    d. a program to raise the political consciousness of Britons.
    e. the title of a popular radio serial in Depression America.

18. Arnold Schonberg was best known for his

    a. paintings that illustrated Socialist Realism.
    b. experimental atonal musical compositions.
    c. revolutionary new directions in drama and film.
    d. Theory of the Collective Unconscious.
    e. use of "stream of consciousness" dialogue in his novels.

19. Characteristic of Nazi Art was the use of

    a. abstract figures to reflect the New Order.
    b. architectural plans designed by the Bauhaus School.
    c. realistic scenes to glorify the strong and the heroic.
    d. an open and public display of human sexuality.
    e. Freudian themes to display the alienation of mankind.

20. Werner Heisenberg is best known for

    a. proposing the theory that uncertainty lies at the bottom of all physical laws.
    b. being on the international scientific team that split the atom.
    c. resurrecting the predictability of Newtonian physics.
    d. the final development of the Atomic Bomb.
    e. warning fellow scientists that they could easily destroy the world.

Complete the Following Sentences:

1. Although Woodrow Wilson originated the idea of a _____ of _____, his country's failure to join and refusal to honor defensive military alliances left _____ insecure and bitter, determined to keep _____ weak.

2. When Germany could not pay further _____, France occupied the _____ Valley, and Germany then fueled _____ by printing more paper money.

3. John Maynard Keynes argued that unemployment stemmed from decline in _____ and that this could be remedied by _____ _____ projects, which could be financed by _____ _____.

4. The French Popular Front introduced new benefit programs for the _____ class, sometimes called the French _____ _____.

5. Benito Mussolini moved in his career from _____ _____ teacher to editor of _____ to founder of the _____ Party.

6. In order to create their perfect Aryan state, the Nazis built death camps for the _____, controlled the population with secret police directed by _____ _____, and trained children for Nazi service in the _____ _____.

7. By 1929 Stalin had secured power in Russia by eliminating all Old _____ from the Politburo, particularly _____ _____, who was eventually murdered at Stalin's orders in _____ in 1940.

8. Totalitarian states used recreation to mold their populations into willing servants of the leader, as is seen in the Fascist _____ and the Nazi _____ _____ _____.

9. The rebellious art movement called Dadaism tried to show the _____ of life by creating what it called _____ – _____, while the _____ Movement sought to visualize the _____.

10. In his masterpiece _____, the Irish exile James Joyce demonstrated the use of a literary "stream of _____" that would become a part of modern literature, featuring ordinary characters from his native city _____.

Place the Following in Chronological Order and Give Dates:

1. *Kristallnacht*   1.

2. Hitler dictatorship established in Germany   2.

3. Fascist dictatorship established in Italy   3.

4. National Government established in Britain   4.

5. Popular Front formed in France   5.

6. New Deal begun in the United States   6.

7. Stalin dictatorship established in Russia   7.

Questions for Critical Thought

1. Explain why the period 1924-1929 was called "The Hopeful Years." What were the hopes, and how were they later dashed?

2. What caused the Great Depression, and how did it change history? How did the various Western democracies react and respond differently to it? Explain why their reactions and responses were so varied.

3. Describe Italy's turn to Fascism. What conditions made it possible, and what role did Mussolini play in it? How did this choice change Italy?

4. Discuss the Nazi movement and its rise to power. What part did Adolf Hitler play in it? What kind of state and society did the National Socialists build?

5. Describe the Fascist and Nazi use of media, leisure programs, and youth organizations to promote their programs. How successful were these schemes? Why and why not?

6. What happened in the Soviet Union between the wars? What role did Stalin play? How does this era help explain Russia's subsequent history?

7. What forms did art and architecture adopt during the years between the wars? How were these forms reflections of the times?

8. Explain the effects of Freud's idea of the "unconscious" on art, music, and literature just before World War II. How long lasting have these effects been in the fields?

Analysis of Primary Source Documents

1. Describe the social effects of unemployment during the Great Depression. How did fascist politicians and military leaders use these conditions to gain popular support?

2. Compare the Pilgrim Trust report on unemployment to the description of Depression life by George Orwell. What common images and problems do you find?

3. From the article supposedly penned by Mussolini, what principles of Italian fascism obviously found their way into the ideology of German Nazism? What was there about fascism that posed threats to internal minorities and to world peace?

4. Analyze Hitler's reaction to seeing the Jew in Vienna. What do his words reveal about his personality? Why do you think this one event left such an impression on him?

5. Combining Hitler's public comments and an observer's description of a Nazi rally, why do you think such mass meetings were so successful? On what human emotions and needs did they play, and why did they lead to such mass support for Hitler's causes?

6. Explain how the Soviet collective farm worked and why there was continual resistance to it by peasants.

7. What picture of Nazi leisure trips do you get from S.D.P. reports? How do these "opposition in exile" reports betray their own biases against the regime?

8. Describe how Hermann Hesse's young character wrestles with his unknown self. Why was this struggle so widely read by young Americans during the 1960's?

CHAPTER TWENTY-SEVEN

THE DEEPENING OF THE EUROPEAN CRISIS: WORLD WAR II

Chapter Outline

I.   Prelude to War (1933-1939)
    A.   Role of Hitler
        1.   Doctrine of *Lebensraum*
        2.   Russia's Perceived Weaknesses
        3.   Racial Supremacy and Empire
    B.   "Diplomatic Revolution" (1933-1936)
        1.   Hitler's "Peaceful" Goals
        2.   Repudiation of the Versailles Treaty
        3.   Occupation of the Rhineland
        4.   Alliance with Mussolini's Italy
    C.   Path to War in Europe (1937-1939)
        1.   Annexation of Austria
        2.   Czechoslovakia and "Munich"
        3.   Invasion of Poland
    D.   Path to War in Asia (1931-1937)
        1.   Japan Seizes Manchuria
        2.   Japan and Germany

II.   Course of World War II
    A.   Victory and Stalemate (1939-1941)
        1.   Blitzkrieg and the British at Dunkirk
        2.   Fall of France and the Vichy Government
        3.   Winston Churchill
        4.   Battle of Britain
        5.   German Invasion of Russia
        6.   War in Asia (Pearl Harbor)
    B.   Turning Point (1942-1943)
        1.   Germany's Defeat at Stalingrad
        2.   Japan's Defeat at Midway
    C.   Last Years of the War (1944-1945)
        1.   Allied Victories in North Africa and Italy
        2.   Allied Invasion of France on D-Day
        3.   Russian Victories in the East
        4.   Germany's Surrender
        5.   Hiroshima and the Surrender of Japan

III. Nazi New Order
    A.   Nazi Empire
        1.   Conquest of "Inferior" Peoples
        2.   New Resources in the East
        3.   Use of Foreign Labor

B. Resistance Movements
    1. Tito in Yugoslavia
    2. De Gaulle and the Free French
    3. Communists
    4. Plot to Kill Hitler
C. Holocaust
    1. Aryan Supremacy
    2. Emigration: The Madagascar Plan
    3. Final Solution: Death Camps
    4. Concentration Camps: Experimentation and Death
    5. Gypsies, Slavs, and Homosexuals
D. New Order in Asia

IV. Home Front
A. Mobilization of Peoples
    1. Planned Economy for Britain
    2. Complete centralization in the Soviet Empire
    3. Partial Mobilization of the American Economy
    4. Late Total Mobilization in Germany
    5. Japanese Patterns
B. Frontline Civilians: Bombing of Cities
    1. Attack on London
    2. British Retaliation against German Cities
    3. Bombing of Japan and Atomic Attack

V. Aftermath of the War: Emergence of the Cold War
A. Wartime Allied Conferences
    1. Teheran and Percentages of Political Influence
    2. Yalta and Roosevelt's Ideal of Self-Determination
    3. Potsdam and Growing Mistrust
    4. Churchill's "Iron Curtain" Speech

Chapter Summary

World War II was the eruption of long simmering animosities and frustrations; and its outcome, both decisive and ambiguous, determined the course of European history for fifty more years. It was also the only truly world war in human history, and it set the global agenda for the remainder of the twentieth century.

The one person most responsible for the war was Adolf Hitler. Germany's bitterness over the outcome of the First World War was present without Hitler, as was a vacuum of power in Eastern Europe, as were Germany's industrial might and capacity to wage war; but Hitler and his Nazi Party gave voice and direction to German's anger, power, and insecurity. Understanding how reluctant the democracies were to fight another war so soon after the last one, Hitler moved to enlarge the frontiers of his Third Reich until his aggression was no longer tolerable.

The first two years of the war, following the invasion of Poland in September, 1939, belonged to the Axis nations: Germany, Italy, and Japan. All the major victories were theirs. Not until early in 1942, with America at last officially allied with Britain and the Soviet Union, did the war turn. After Hitler's failure in Russia, after Italy's failure to resist Allied forces from North Africa, after the United States gained sea superiority against Japan, after the Allies successfully invaded France, the war ground to its deadly conclusion.

The Nazi Empire had done its bloody worst in all the lands it had held. Despite the effectiveness of resistance movements everywhere, Nazi forces dominated much of the continent for five years, bringing oppression and death to Jews, minorities, and all "inferior" peoples. Indiscriminate bombing of civilian areas by both sides led to a tragic number of innocent deaths. World War II was costly in every way.

Even before the surrender of Germany and Japan, the victors had trouble agreeing on the post-war world; and at the various conferences called to determine borders and governments it was evident that a separation between East and West was inevitable. World War II ended almost as tragically as World War I. The Cold War began.

Learning Objectives

1. Be able to explain Hitler's early successes on the diplomatic front and how he was able to prepare for war without strong enough opposition from the democracies.

2. Trace the path to war both in Europe and in Asia, and point out the mistakes the democracies made in their treatment of Hitler.

3. Describe the Nazi Empire, its structure and policies, and show how Hitler's philosophy formed and directed it, particularly the treatment of the Jews.

4. Show how the war affected civilian populations and how governments mobilized their people to help win the war.

5. Discuss the events and attitudes near the end of the war that precipitated the Cold War that followed it.

Glossary of Names and Terms

1. *Lebensraum*: Hitler's term to describe the geographical space, mostly to the east, that Germany needed to expand and satisfy its people's demands.

2. *Sudetenland*: Hitler's term for the parts of Czechoslovakia that was home to ethnic Germans, whom he wanted to bring into the Third Reich.

3. Vichy: the small resort town in southern France that became the capital of the French puppet regime under World War I general Henri Pétain.

4. El Alamein: site in North Africa where British forces stopped the German advance under Rommel in the summer of 1942.

5. Midway: island where American planes destroyed four Japanese aircraft carriers and established U.S. superiority in the Pacific in 1942.

6. Josip Broz: known as Tito, he led the Yugoslavian resistance to Nazi occupation and later became leader of his country.

7. Holocaust: the Nazi systematic genocide of the Jewish populations in the countries they conquered and occupied.

8. Hiroshima: Japanese city, relatively unscarred by the war before 1945, where the United States dropped the first atomic bomb.

9. Cold War: the war of nerves between East and West, led by the U.S.S.R. and the U.S. A., which dominated world politics from 1945 to 1990.

10. Iron Curtain: Winston Churchill's term for the sealed border that separated Soviet-occupied lands in Eastern Europe from the Western democracies.

Match These Words with Their Definitions:

1.	Munich	A.	Designed to implement the Final Solution
2.	Dunkirk	B.	Where Germany's Sixth Army was lost
3.	Stalingrad	C.	Completely destroyed by British bombing
4.	Midway	D.	Worst British defeat of the war
5.	Madagascar	E.	Confirmed post-war mistrust among the Allies
6.	Auschwitz	F.	Gave the United States supremacy in the Pacific
7.	Coventry	G.	Created the United Nations
8.	Dresden	H.	Proposed as site for resettlement of European Jews
9.	Yalta	I.	Completely destroyed by German bombing
10.	Potsdam	J.	Confirmed Hitler's belief that the democracies were weak

Choose the Correct Answer:

1. World War II was largely caused by

   a. Britain's arrogant behavior toward Germany.
   b. the instability of the French government.
   c. Soviet expansionism and its threat to Western European security.
   d. ill advised actions of the League of Nations.
   e. a power vacuum in Central Europe that Germany sought to fill.

2. When Hitler came to power, Germany was

   a. militarily the most powerful state in Europe.
   b. limited by the Treaty of Versailles to an army of 100,000.
   c. threatening the independence of Poland and Czechoslovakia.
   d. already massing troops in the Rhineland.
   e. unspeakably poor both in natural resources and men of fighting age.

3.   The British policy of appeasement toward Hitler was based on

     a.   the effete nature of the British upper class.
     b.   admiration for the Germans and their culture.
     c.   hatred and distrust of the French.
     d.   the conviction that it would maintain stability and peace.
     e.   an inability of the elective system to form a stable government.

4.   Winston Churchill concluded that the Munich Conference was

     a.   proof that the Chamberlain government was "wise and prudent."
     b.   successful in keeping the Germans out of the Sudetenland.
     c.   a failure that set a bad precedent.
     d.   a severe political setback for Hitler at home.
     e.   only the first step toward normalizing relations with Hitler.

5.   Following the Allied evacuation at Dunkirk, France

     a.   soon surrendered, and Germany established the Vichy government.
     b.   went on the offensive and stopped Germany in Normandy.
     c.   called on Italy to help them fight the Germans.
     d.   appealed to F.D.R. to enter the war.
     e.   brought Hitler's actions to the attention of the League of Nations.

6.   The Grand Alliance of World War II made its first goal the

     a.   defeat of Japan and Germany.
     b.   unconditional surrender of Germany.
     c.   liberation of African colonies taken by Germany.
     d.   liberation of Asian colonies taken by Japan.
     e.   occupation of France and neutralization of Britain.

7.   The war in North Africa was best characterized by

     a.   the overwhelming superiority of Italian troops.
     b.   the overwhelming superiority of German troops.
     c.   strong German lines of supply that lengthened the conflict.
     d.   heavy fighting only around oases.
     e.   allied persistence despite initial German victories.

8.   The turning point of the North African campaign came when

     a.   British stopped Rommel at El Alamein in the summer of 1942.
     b.   South African troops allied themselves with the British.
     c.   the Free French revolted against the Vichy regime in Algeria.
     d.   the Italians changed sides and joined the Allies in the fall of 1942.
     e.   Egyptian resistance fighters assassinated four major German generals.

9.   After the attack on Pearl Harbor, the priority of the United States was to

   a.   get revenge on Japan as quickly as possible.
   b.   recover the Hawaiian Islands and Philippines.
   c.   defeat Germany and then turn all of its resources against Japan.
   d.   buy time to build back its industrial and military supplies.
   e.   free its soldiers held in Japanese prison of war camps.

10. Hitler's grand plan would have made the Slavic peoples

   a.   into one nation trained to fight the Russians.
   b.   slaves working on the land grants of triumphant Germans.
   c.   low ranking soldiers in the army of the Third Reich.
   d.   the richest farmers in the world.
   e.   learn German and become citizens of the Third Reich.

11. Hitler's intentions for his land conquests in Eastern Europe included

   a.   making the area one giant timber and mining region.
   b.   setting up a puppet Slavic state as a buffer against Russia.
   c.   sending Germans to colonize the area as land holders.
   d.   the creation of a wildlife preserve with game keepers the only settlers.
   e.   establishing a plantation where he could retire in 1950.

12. The turning point in the war for Eastern Europe was the

   a.   German fiasco at Stalingrad.
   b.   German victory at Leningrad.
   c.   Russian victory at Kiev.
   d.   Russian fiasco at Moscow.
   e.   German withdrawal from Warsaw.

13. American naval superiority in the Pacific was

   a.   never in question, even days after Pearl Harbor.
   b.   precarious throughout the war and not assured until 1945.
   c.   achieved beyond dispute by the Battle of Midway.
   d.   irrelevant because the Americans had no intentions of fighting a naval war.
   e.   unnecessary because of superior American air power.

14. The Allied advance through Italy was

   a.   extremely slow due to staunch Italian resistance.
   b.   extremely rapid with all of Italy taken by November 1943.
   c.   greatly aided by Soviet troops invading from the north.
   d.   quite slow due to the effectiveness of German defenses.
   e.   put on hold in 1943 in order to invade the Third Reich.

15. The Nazi Empire was

    a. organized into efficiently operating bureaus.
    b. never much larger than Germany and Austria.
    c. never very well organized or efficiently governed.
    d. composed of independent states that willingly cooperated with Hitler.
    e. held together by the common Aryan philosophies of all its constituent states.

16. Nazi rule was most ruthless in

    a. Eastern Europe where the Slavs were considered racial inferiors.
    b. France because of the age-old rivalry between the Germans and the French.
    c. Denmark and the Netherlands because they were so geographically near Germany.
    d. Italy because the Germans did not trust them as competent allies.
    e. Austria because its Catholic population resented being part of a Protestant state.

17. A major source of resistance to the Nazis across Western Europe came from

    a. German citizens, who considered Hitler an embarrassment.
    b. Communists, especially after the Nazi invasion of Russia.
    c. the Vichy French, who were the bravest of the Allies.
    d. the Austrians, who believed they were the true Aryans.
    e. the papacy, which officially condemned Nazi thought in 1939.

18. Nazi atrocities at Auschwitz

    a. are now regarded as fiction distributed after the war by Jews and Communists.
    b. were willingly carried out by SS men who had few qualms about killing.
    c. were limited to Jews, with other despised groups sent to work camps.
    d. included cruel and painful "medical" experiments on inmates.
    e. far exceeded those at any other concentration camp.

19. Civilian bombing was carried out mainly to

    a. reduce the number of men available for military service.
    b. reduce the number of women available to work in factories.
    c. break the will of average people to resist.
    d. reach goals set by ministries of war for body counts.
    e. get revenge for earlier bombings of arms factories.

20. The official reason given for dropping the atomic bomb on Japan was to

    a. punish Japan for the bombing of Pearl Harbor.
    b. test it out for later use against Germany.
    c. compensate for the lack of conventional weapons in the U.S. arsenal.
    d. to save the American lives that a land invasion of Japan would cost.
    e. prove American superiority in science and technology.

Complete the Following Sentences:

1. In 1936 Hitler's army occupied the _____, and in 1938 he annexed _____. Later
    that year he cast his eyes toward what he called Germany's _____.

2. At Munich, Chamberlain followed a policy of _____ toward Hitler, which in effect gave him a green light to invade _____.

3. After the Nazi invasion of _____ led to World War II, Hitler used "lightning war" or in German _____ to take Denmark, Norway, Netherlands, Belgium, and finally in June, 1940, _____.

4. While Germany occupied three-fifths of France, Marshal _____ was permitted to establish a _____ government for the rest of the country, with a capital at the resort town of _____.

5. World War II started in Asia in 1937 when Japan invaded _____; and in July, 1941, the United States placed trade sanctions against Japan for occupying _____; but war between Japan and the U.S. started with Japan's bombing of _____ _____ on December 7, 1941.

6. In 1942 the Allies stopped Rommel in _____ _____; the German army failed to take the Russian city of _____; and the U.S. defeated Japan in the Battle of _____ _____.

7. After Hitler invaded Russia, _____ all across Europe began leading movements of resistance to Nazism, but within Germany all resistance, such as the White _____ movement, were brutally crushed by the _____.

8. While early suggestions such as the _____ Plan would have sent European Jews into exile, the Final Solution as carried out by S.S. Security Service head _____ _____ was systematic _____.

9. The only World War II country to use women in combat, _____ _____, trained female bomber pilots, who became known as _____ _____.

10. Convinced that an invasion of Japan might cause a million _____ deaths, U.S. President Harry Truman ordered an atomic bomb dropped first on _____ and then on _____, ending the war.

Place the Following in Chronological Order and Give Dates:

1. German surrender at Stalingrad   1.

2. U.S. drops an atomic bomb on Hiroshima   2.

3. Battle of Britain   3.

4. German occupation of the Rhineland   4.

5. Allied invasion of France   5.

6. German invasion of Poland   6.

7. Japanese attack Pearl Harbor   7.

Questions for Critical Thought

1. Describe the "diplomatic revolution" that Hitler began after 1933. Explain how this revolution led eventually to war.

2. Trace the steps to war between 1935 and 1939. Who were the major figures in the drama, and what part did each one play?

3. Tell the story of the first two years of World War II. If you had been reporting from the field in October 1942, what would you have predicted? Why?

4. Explain why late 1942-1943 was the "turning point" of World War II. What people and events helped make it so?

5. Describe the Nazi Empire: its organization, what it sought to accomplish, and its relative success. How does the Holocaust fit into the overall picture?

6. Compare and contrast the way Britain, Russia, Germany and America mobilized their civilian populations for the war effort. What effects did each one's plan have on the outcome?

7. Describe what it was like to live in a "front line" city during the war. To what extent did bombing affect the outcome of the war?

8. By reviewing the Big Three wartime conferences, show why participants should have foreseen the Cold War. Where exactly were crucial mistakes made—and by whom?

Analysis of Primary Source Documents

1. What did Hitler mean by "sufficient living space" for Germany? Where did his vision lead him and his nation?

2. Compare and contrast the two interpretations—by Churchill and Chamberlain—of the Munich agreement. At that moment in history, which sounded the more plausible? Explain.

3. Using the German soldier's diary, explain how and why the German army in Russia lost heart. Why did this man not blame his leader for the fiasco?

4. Describe Hitler's vision of the new society he would establish in Eastern Europe. How was it to be achieved? What were its strengths and weaknesses?

5. Recount the systematic way people at German extermination camps were dispatched. What ideology and reasoning stood behind such a system?

6. How did aerial bombing change the nature and character of war? Describe its effects on people in cities under bombardment.

7. Show how the statements by Churchill and Stalin in March, 1946, illustrate the mutual mistrust that shaped the Cold War.

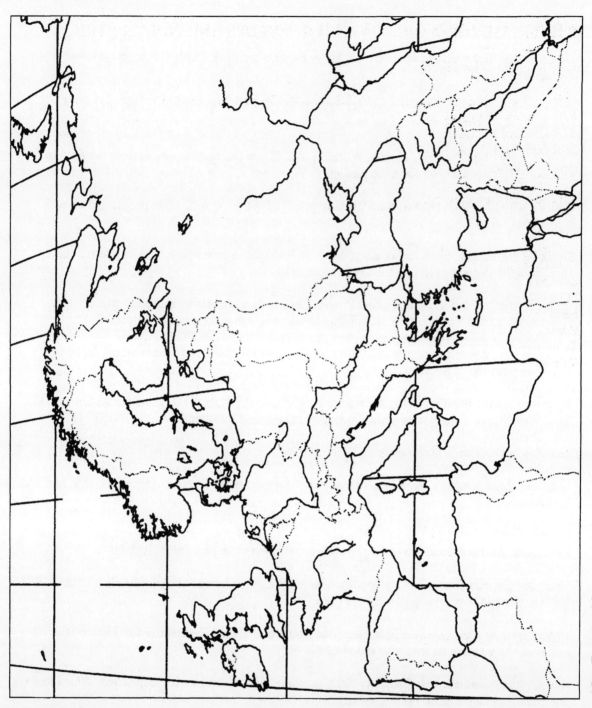

Map Exercise 16

MAP EXERCISE 16: WORLD WAR II IN EUROPE AND NORTH AFRICA

Shade and label the following:

1. Allied powers Britain, Portugal, the U.S.S.R., the Middle East, and areas under allied control
2. Axis powers—Germany and Italy
3. Axis satellites and allies
4. Conquests made by Axis 1939-1942
5. Neutral nations

Pinpoint and label the following:

1. Algiers
2. Berlin
3. Casablanca
4. London
5. Moscow
6. Paris
7. Rome
8. Tunis
9. Warsaw

CHAPTER TWENTY-EIGHT

COLD WAR AND A NEW WESTERN WORLD, 1945-1973

Chapter Outline

I. Development of the Cold War
    A. Confrontation of the Superpowers
        1. Differing Historical Perspectives
        2. Disagreement over Eastern Europe
        3. Greece, Turkey, and the Truman Doctrine
        4. Western Europe and the Marshall Plan
        5. Policy of Containment
        6. Berlin and the Airlift
        7. NATO and the Warsaw Pact
    B. Global Cold War
        1. Korean Conflict
        2. Escalation of the Cold War
        3. Berlin Again
        4. Cuban Missile Crisis and Détente
            a. Fidel Castro's Cuba
            b. Kennedy, Khrushchev, and Crisis
        3. U.S. Involvement in Vietnam
        4. Steps toward Better Relations between the Superpowers

II. Europe and the World: Decolonization
    A. Africa: Struggle for Independence
    B. Conflict in the Middle East
        1. Nasser and Pan-Arabism
        2. Arab-Israeli Dispute
    C. Asia: Nationalism and Communism
    D. Decolonization and Cold War Rivalries

III. Recovery and Renewal in Europe
    A. Soviet Union: From Stalin to Khrushchev
        1. Economic Recovery
        2. Military Buildup and Technological Advance
        3. Khrushchev and Destabilization
        4. Eastern Europe: Behind the Iron Curtain
            a. Albania and Yugoslavia
            b. Upheaval in Eastern Europe
    B. Western Europe's Revival of Democracy and the Economy
        1. France and Charles De Gaulle
            a. Algerian Crisis and End of the Fourth Republic
            b. De Gaulle and the Fifth Republic
        2. West Germany
            a. Konrad Adenauer and Rearmament
            b. Ludwig Erhard and Economic Recovery
            c. Denazification

Chapter Summary

No sooner did the Allies defeat the Central Powers than they began bickering among themselves. The democracies hoped to see a Europe of representative governments and free markets, while the Soviets wanted to create a buffer against further threats from the West. What Winston Churchill called an Iron Curtain descended across the continent, separating East from West. The Cold War began.

Distrust grew as each side came to see the other as a menace to safety in the world. The Cold War, made all the more dangerous by the presence on both sides of nuclear weapons, continued through much of the rest of the twentieth century, dominating foreign policy in all European countries. Only after the Cuban Missile Crisis of 1963, when world survival hung in the balance, did the two sides take the first tentative steps toward détente.

Meanwhile the face of Europe was changed in the years just after the war. The old European empires collapsed, and their colonies became politically if not always economically independent. Now free to experiment with social reform, many of the Western democracies created welfare states, providing social security, health care, and pensions for their citizens. Western Europe grouped together militarily in the North Atlantic Treaty Organization and economically in the organization of the Common Market.

European society changed during the period from 1945 to 1973. Citizen protests of the status quo occurred on both sides of the Iron Curtain. In Hungary and in Czechoslovakia of the Soviet bloc, in France and the United States of the West, people protested materialism and injustice. Everywhere in the

West there was more freedom than in the past, as consumerism held sway, as women and minorities pressed for equal treatment. Yet there was also a feeling that society had lost its way, and some called it a permissive society.

People looked for new solutions to new problems. While art and literature continued down their experimental pathways, while the philosophy of existentialism tried to answer the questions modern people asked, there was a noticeable revival of interest in religion, and American culture expanded its influence globally.

Learning Objectives

1. Be able to trace the history of the Cold War from its inception through the attempts at détente in the early 1970s.

2. Explain why the European nations shed their colonies after the war, and show how decolonization affected both Europe and the parts of the world where their colonies were free.

3. Describe the major events in the Soviet Empire during this period, and show they affected politics in the democracies.

4. Discuss the emergence of the United States as a super power and how it reacted to global challenges in its new role.

5. Describe post war culture, and show how art, literature, philosophy, and religion both reflected and molded it.

Glossary of Names and Terms

1. Truman Doctrine: American promise to aid legitimate governments resisting Communist uprisings, in the first case Greece and Turkey.

2. NATO: North Atlantic Treaty Organization, founded to protest Western Europe from Soviet aggression.

3. Bay of Pigs: sit in Cuba where invaders bent on overthrowing the Communist leader Fidel Castro were taken prisoner, hastening the Cuban Missile Crisis.

4. Ho Chi Minh: Communist leader of the independence movement in Vietnam and symbol of resistance to the U.S. attempt to prop up a pro-western state in the south of the country.

5. African National Congress: organization founded in 1912, which was dedicated at first to rights for Africans under colonial governments and later to African independence.

6. Gamal Abdel Nasser: leader of Egypt who successfully nationalized the Suez Canal and became leader of the movement toward Pan-Arabism.

7. Mao Zedong: Communist leader who after decades of civil war with the Nationalists emerged victorious and established the People's Republic of China in 1949.

8. Charles De Gaulle: retired general who returned to the political arena to establish and become the first president of the Fifth French Republic.

9.   Simone de Beauvoir: most important postwar European spokeswoman for feminism, charging in her book *The Second Sex* that women had been taught to think of themselves as "the Other."

10.   Jackson Pollock: painter whose enormous canvases escaped completely the traditional definition of art as representing visual reality.

Match These Words with Their Definitions:

1.   Truman Doctrine

2.   Marshall Plan

3.   CENTO

4.   SEATO

5.   Sputnik

6.   Alexander Solzhenitsyn

7.   Josip Broz

8.   Alexander Dubcek

9.   Charles de Gaulle

10.   Herbert Marcuse

A.   Designed to save Asian countries from Chinese Communism

B.   Publication of his novels demonstrated some liberalization in Russia

C.   First artificial earth satellite

D.   Designed to prevent Communist aggression in Greece and Turkey

E.   Leader of resistance to Nazis who later ruled Yugoslavia

F.   Founder of the Fifth French Republic

G.   Designed to save the Middle East from Russian aggression

H.   Critic of capitalism who hoped for a student revolution

I.   Restored Western Europe's economy

J.   Removed by a Soviet show of force

Choose the Correct Answer:

1.   The Truman Doctrine, that promised aid to countries resisting Communist domination, came in response to

   a.   insurgencies within Greece and Turkey.
   b.   Soviet designs on Austria.
   c.   East German threats to West Germany.
   d.   North Korean threats to South Korea.
   e.   insurgencies within Britain and France.

2.   The American plan to aid Europe's economic recovery was designed by

   a.   Secretary of State Dean Acheson.
   b.   Secretary of State George Marshall.
   c.   President Harry Truman.
   d.   President Dwight D. Eisenhower.
   e.   *Foreign Affairs* editor George Kennan.

3. The Cold War struggle over Germany resulted in

    a. the creation of an independent, united Germany under Walter Ulbricht.
    b. an East German economic miracle brought about with Soviet technological advances.
    c. a successful blockade of West Berlin by Soviet forces.
    d. the creation of two separate German states.
    e. several near nuclear exchanges along the Rhine.

4. During the Korean War, American General Douglas MacArthur was leader of

    a. an army made up of South Korean volunteers.
    b. forces authorized and manned by the United Nations.
    c. the American Eighth Army.
    d. NATO forces sent to aid South Korea.
    e. the newly reformed Empire of Japan.

5. One overall effect of the Korean War was

    a. the domination of Southeast Asia by the United States.
    b. an end to American and Soviet involvement in Asian affairs.
    c. the reinforcement of American determination to contain Soviet power in the world.
    d. an end to all Communist efforts to gain a foothold on the Asian continent.
    e. the reelection of President Harry Truman.

6. The Berlin Wall

    a. was built to keep Soviet troops from invading Berlin.
    b. was a powerful symbol of a divided Germany and Europe.
    c. surrounded the entire city of Berlin.
    d. remained in place for fifteen years.
    e. prevented all escapes from Soviet occupied lands.

7. In 1962 President Kennedy responded to proof that there were nuclear weapons in Cuba with

    a. an order to keep it secret so as not to disturb the American public until he could act.
    b. an order to invade the island, which failed at the Bay of Pigs.
    c. a blockade of the island which required Soviet ships to return to Russia.
    d. an air attack that knocked out most of the missiles.
    e. a boycott of all U.S. trade with Russia.

8. The Cuban Missile Crisis resulted in

    a. the fall of the Stalin government.
    b. the installation of Soviet missiles in other Caribbean locales.
    c. an attempt by Miami-based Cubans to overthrow the Castro regime.
    d. President Kennedy's secret agreement to a number of Khrushchev's demands.
    e. an improvement in communications between the U.S. and the U.S.S.R.

9. Post-World War II life in the U.S.S.R. under Stalin saw

   a. continued low standards of living for the working classes.
   b. an emphasis on the production of luxury consumer goods.
   c. relaxation of restrictions on artists and writers.
   d. the adaptation of Communist programs to new Western European ways.
   e. peasants adapt at last to collectivization.

10. The domestic policy of Nikita Khrushchev in the 1950s and early 1960s

    a. was basically a continuation of Stalin's policies.
    b. was bolstered by his successes in foreign policy.
    c. tried but failed to benefit the Soviet economy and industry.
    d. focused on repressing intellectuals and artists.
    e. demonstrated his inadequate training for the job of premier.

11. The 1956 independence movement in Hungary resulted in

    a. the end of Soviet-style Communist rule there.
    b. an end to American influence in Eastern Europe.
    c. armed Soviet intervention and the reassertion of strong Communist leadership.
    d. a resurgence of the Catholic faith among the Hungarian people.
    e. the emergence for the first time of a Hungarian national pride.

12. The 1968 Czechoslovakian "Prague Spring"

    a. was triggered by the reforms of Alexander Dubcek.
    b. led to the presidency in 1970 of Václav Havel.
    c. saw Czechoslovakia withdraw from the Soviet bloc.
    d. brought about the resignation of Gustav Husak.
    e. made a number of Czech artists and writers world famous.

13. As President of France, Charles de Gaulle's policy toward the Cold War was to

    a. align France with the Warsaw Pact nations.
    b. keep France independent of the superpowers.
    c. follow the American lead throughout.
    d. make France a leading member of NATO.
    e. renounce all economic treaties with Britain.

14. The first chancellor of the German Federal Republic, Konrad Adenauer

    a. followed British leadership on foreign policy.
    b. remained neutral between the two superpowers.
    c. rebuilt the German army as quickly as possible.
    d. sought above all a reconciliation of relations with France.
    e. became America's most trusted ally.

15. Which of the following statements about postwar Britain is *false*?

    a.   National Insurance and National health acts helped make Britain a welfare state.
    b.   The Conservative Party in the 1950s revoked nearly all of the socialist legislation of the Labour Party of the 1940s.
    c.   Neither Labour nor the Conservatives could solve problems of labor, the economy, or Northern Ireland.
    d.   Churchill served a second term before retiring.
    e.   The Suez Crisis proved that Britain could not successfully oppose America's will.

16. Post-war Italian politics were characterized by

    a.   the increasing dominance of the Communist Party.
    b.   the demise of the Christian Democrats.
    c.   a persistent call for a fascist restoration.
    d.   constant interference in domestic affairs by the Pope.
    e.   chronic instability due to the necessity of parliamentary coalitions.

17. The Common Market began by

    a.   building a multinational supersonic aircraft.
    b.   adopting a common currency for trade purposes.
    c.   dropping trade barriers on coal and steel products.
    d.   refusing to agree to the U.S. application for membership.
    e.   rejecting the application for membership of any former fascist state.

18. The writings of Simone de Beauvoir

    a.   were used as textbook in most French Catholic girls schools.
    b.   made women aware of their second class status.
    c.   made women aware of the equal rewards of careers and motherhood.
    d.   were seldom translated into other languages because of their philosophical complexities.
    e.   reflected her long time romantic involvement with Jean-Paul Sartre.

19. The outbreak of student revolts in the late 1960s was inspired by

    a.   a growing conviction of the immorality of the war in Vietnam.
    b.   overcrowded classrooms and lack of professional attention.
    c.   discontent with the increasing materialism of Western society.
    d.   all of the above
    e.   none of the above

20. One of the most intriguing elements of Jackson Pollock's art was

    a.   the subtle inclusion of social commentary.
    b.   high price his sculpture brought from the 1950s onward.
    c.   the debt it owed to Asian art.
    d.   his ability to paint portraits and abstract works with equal ease.
    e.   his unusual method, influenced by Native American artists.

Complete the Following Sentences:

1. U.S. President Truman was so alarmed in 1947 by _____ inability to defend the eastern Mediterranean that he offered American aid to protect _____ and _____ against Soviet expansion.

2. U.S. diplomat George Kennan, an expert in _____ affairs, influenced American policy for decades with his article in _____ _____ calling for _____ of Communism.

3. President Kennedy's response to discovering Soviet _____ in Cuba in 1962 was to _____ the island and then agree not to _____ it.

4. After _____ _____ led his communists to power in China, the government collectivized all _____ _____ and nationalized most _____ and _____.

5. Khrushchev's criticism of _____ encouraged such a spirit of rebellion in the Soviet _____ that he had to crush a 1956 uprising in _____ and one in 1968 in _____.

6. When Imry Nagy declared _____ a free nation and threatened Soviet control by promising elections, the _____ _____ occupied the capital city, _____.

7. To make the case that France was in the 1950s still a great power, Charles de Gaulle withdrew from _____, built his own _____ weapons, and increased the production and export of _____ and _____.

8. When Ludwig Erhard's work as Minister of Finance for West Germany helped bring about the post-war _____ _____," voters chose him to succeed _____ _____ as chancellor.

9. The British welfare system, which inspired other European nations, nationalized the _____ of England, enacted a National _____ Act, and established a National _____ Service.

10. The Common Market, established in 1957 when _____ European nations signed the _____ Treaty, eliminated customs barriers and created a _____ _____ _____.

Place the Following in Chronological Order and Give Dates:

1. Cuban missile crisis   1.

2. Formation of the Warsaw Pact   2.

3. Erection of the Berlin Wall   3.

4. Formation of NATO   4.

5. The Prague Spring   5.

6. Truman Doctrine outlined   6.

7. De Gaulle assumes power in France   7.

Questions for Critical Thought

1. What were the causes of the Cold War? What issues divided East and West? Did world leaders during the 1950s and 1960s make things better or worse?

2. Trace the American response to Communism from the Truman Doctrine through the Cuban Missile Crisis. What part did the theories of George Kennan play in the formulation of American policy?

3. How did "decolonization" affect both the First World and the Third World? What kind of world would we have today had it all been slower, better planned, and more peaceful?

4. Trace the history of the Soviet Bloc from 1945 to 1970. To what degree did its rivalry with the West create its policies and shape its development? How did it in turn affect the policies and development of the West?

5. Explain Charles de Gaulle's foreign policy. How and why was it so different from that of most Western nations?

6. What areas of the citizen's life were affected by the experiments in the welfare state adopted by Western democracies after World War II? What are the benefits and problems of the welfare state?

7. Describe West Germany's attempt to establish a place in the European community of nations after the war. What difficulties did it face, and well did it deal with them? What accounts for its "economic miracle?"

8. Discuss the causes and effects of the "permissive" society of post-war Europe. In what ways does it still affect Western life today?

Analysis of Primary Source Documents

1. Give the major thrust of the Truman Doctrine. What threat provoked it, what was its intent, and where did it lead? What similar threats later appeared, and how did subsequent presidents respond to them?

2. Compare Khrushchev's account of the Cuban Missile Crisis with what you know of the American version of this event. Who was really the aggressor, and who really won the standoff?

3. How does Franz Fanon's murder case demonstrate the brutalization of youth by social unrest? Name places in today's world where the same thing could happen.

4. What made Khrushchev denounce Stalin, the man he had served? What did his candor do for Communist Party credibility?

5. How does the 1956 uprising against Soviet rule in Hungary look today, when Hungary is at last free of foreign domination? What now seems to be its significance? Will today's view continue?

6. Explain what Simone de Beauvoir meant by the "Second Sex" and the "Other." Why do men perpetuate this image, and why do women tolerate it?

7. If Bob Dylan's song is an anthem for the protest movement of the 1960s, what audiences did young people want to reach and why?

8. Compare and contrast the two student proclamations of 1968. How do they reveal both the awareness and the naiveté of the student protest movements of the time?

CHAPTER TWENTY-NINE
THE CONTEMPORARY WESTERN WORLD (SINCE 1973)

Chapter Outline

I.   Toward a New Western Order
    A. Revolutionary Era in the Soviet Union
        1. Mikhail Gorbachev: *Perestroika* and *Glasnost*
        2. Economic Crises and Nationalist Movements
        3. End of the U.S.S.R.
    B. Eastern Europe: Collapse of the Communist Order
        1. Lech Walesa's Solidarity in Poland
        2. Hungary
        3. Vaclav Havel in Czechoslovakia
        4. Romania
        5. Bulgaria
    C. Reunification of Germany
        1. Communist Disarray
        2. Fall of the Berlin Wall
    D. Disintegration of Yugoslavia
        1. Serbian Nationalism
        2. War in Bosnia
        3. Dayton Accords
        4. War in Kosovo
        5. Aftermath
    E. Western Europe: Winds of Change
        1. Germany Restored
        2. Britain and Thatcherism
        3. Uncertainties in France
        4. Confusion in Italy
        5. Unification of Europe
        6. Domestic Turmoil in the United States
        7. Contemporary Canada

II. After the Cold War: New World Order or Age of Terrorism?
    A. Carter's Human Rights and Reagan's "Star Wars"
    B. End of the Cold War
        1. Gorbachev Era
        2. Gulf War Test
    C. An Age of Terrorism?
        1. Terrorist Organizations
        2. Attack on the United States

III. New Directions and New Problems in Western Society
    A. Transformation in Women's Lives
    B. Guest Workers and Immigrants
        1. Ethnic Conflict
        2. Attacks on Foreigners

C. Green Movement
    1. Concern for the Environment
    2. Political Action
D. Trends in Art, Literature, and Music
    1. Postmodernism in Literature: Gabriel García Márquez
    2. Music: Olivier Messiaen's Serialism
E. Science and Technology
    1. Computers
    2. Military Technology
    3. Space Race
    4. "Small is Beautiful" Movement

IV. Toward a Global Civilization?
A. Global Problems
B. Non-governmental Organizations
C. International Cooperation

Chapter Summary

The Western world has seen amazing changes during the past twenty years. The most remarkable of these has been the disintegration of the Soviet Union and the release of its dependent countries. As late as 1980 the Cold War still raged as an ideological struggle between Capitalism and Communism; but by 1990 the entire picture had changed.

Beginning with Mikhail Gorbachev's attempt to reform the Soviet economy, pressure for change gathered such strength that the Soviet Union was dissolved and all the countries that were once a part of its sphere of influence were freed to go their own ways. Germany was reunited, while Yugoslavia crumbled into warring factions. Old enemies became friends in an effort to cope with threats of chaos from many sides, while ethnic groups once forcibly combined under single national banners began pulling apart to create autonomous states. The world about to enter the twenty-first century looked quite different from the one formed just after World War II.

While the "new world order" was still forming, the challenges and problems facing it were already clear. Terrorism sponsored by dissident groups, tensions caused by the presence of alien residents in many countries, and threats to humankind from environmental abuses are the issues to occupy attention and energies for the foreseeable future. New trends in the arts, literature, the sciences, philosophy and religion reflect both the tensions of the Cold War now past and the uncertainties that come with its demise.

It is clear that in order to cope with the dangers and realize the opportunities lying in the future, Western Europeans must begin to think globally. The nation-state, for so long the decisive institution in Western man's life, must take second place to the state of humankind if we are all to live full lives in peace with ourselves and the environment. The heroes of the future may be the men and women who show the way to think and live in this fashion.

Learning Objectives

1. Be able to trace the events that shaped the latter part of the Cold War and those that brought it to an end.

2. Describe the way and explain why the Soviet Union dissolved into its several parts, and explain what effect this had on world affairs.

3. Discuss the way the former Soviet dependencies responded to their independence, and explain why some were brilliant successes while others were dismal failures.

4. Describe the way the western democracies have developed over the past thirty years, and show how they have responded to terrorist threats.

5. Discuss recent trends in culture, including the arts, the sciences, and thoughts about globalism.

Glossary of Names and Terms

1. *Perestroika*: Mikhail Gorbachev's program to restructure the Soviet system, especially the economy, by introducing more liberal policies.

2. *Glasnost*: Gorbachev's attempt to open the Soviet Union to more political, cultural, and intellectual exchanges with the western democracies.

3. Solidarity: Polish labor union, led by Lech Walesa, which succeeded in declaring Polish independence from Soviet control.

4. Vaclav Havel: poet and playwright, often imprisoned for dissidence, who led Czechoslovakia to independence and became its first post-communist president.

5. "Ethnic cleansing": the policy of the Serbs in the former Yugoslavia forcibly to remove Bosnian Muslims from the lands they wanted as part of their new nation.

6. "Iron Lady": name often applied to British Prime Minister Margaret Thatcher, who during the 1980s made strong efforts to reverse the socialist trends of her country.

7. Eurocommunism: name given to the attempt of some Western European communists after the fall of the Soviet Union to broaden their appeal by dropping the more radical elements of Marxism.

8. "Star Wars": Common name for the U.S. Strategic Defense Initiative, promoted by Ronald Reagan, to build a space shield against missile attack.

9. Grace Hopper: career naval officer who invented COBOL, a system that enabled computers to respond to words as well as to numbers.

10. E.F. Schumacher: author whose works encouraged conservative of resources, arguing that "small is beautiful."

Match These Words with Their Definitions:

1. *Perestroika*

A.   Site of NATO bombings

2. Lech Walesa

B.   Site of first U.S.-U.S.S.R. cooperative effort

3. Vaclav Havel

C.   Combined optimism with fantasy

4. Kosovo

D.   Leader of Solidarity

5. Watergate

E.   Argued for downsizing

6. Kuwait

F.   Used chants, folk, and birdsongs

7. Chernobyl

G.   Playwright turned president

8. Milan Kundera

H.   Great aid to the Green Movement

9. Olivier Messiaen

I.   Brought down a democratically elected president

10. E.F. Schumacher

J.   Plan for solving Soviet domestic problems

Choose the Correct Answer:

1. Mikhail Gorbachev's plan of *perestroika* at first aimed at a

    a.   market economy with complete free enterprise and homestead lands.
    b.   market economy with some free enterprise and some private property.
    c.   modified Marxism with the state controlling all businesses.
    d.   return to pure Marxism, which he believed had been too quickly abandoned.
    e.   creating small free enterprise zones in inner cities.

2. Gorbachev was surprised when his *glasnost* was effectively used by

    a.   military officers to gain even more power.
    b.   religious leaders to restore their old privileges.
    c.   ethnic and national groups to press for more autonomy.
    d.   the old Communist guard to retain powers they were losing to democracy.
    e.   underworld figures to create a Russian mafia.

3. Leader of Solidarity Lech Walesa

    a.   rose to prominence as a labor leader.
    b.   depended heavily on the support of the Catholic Church.
    c.   became the first president of the new Polish Republic.
    d.   was defeated for president by a former communist.
    e.   all of the above

4. In Romania the move to overthrow the Communist regime in 1989 ended with Chairman Ceausescu and his wife being

    a.   sent into exile in the Soviet Union.
    b.   sentenced to life in prison for their corruption.
    c.   sent to work on a communal farm in Bosnia.
    d.   tried and executed.
    e.   permitted to seek asylum in the United States.

5. With German reunification in 1990, the section that was the former East Germany

    a.   became known as Middle Germany.
    b.   was the richest part of the new nation.
    c.   ceased to exist as a separate entity.
    d.   kept its own legislature and currency.
    e.   had little trouble being absorbed into the new nation.

6. After Tito's death in 1980, Yugoslavia was plunged into civil war by Serbian demands for

    a.   the reestablishment of the Catholic Church in Bosnia.
    b.   new expanded borders to accommodate Serb minorities.
    c.   repayment of loans made by the World Bank.
    d.   separate membership in NATO.
    e.   all Muslims to be expelled from Yugoslavian territories.

7. Margaret Thatcher's popularity rose when she successfully prevented

    a.   Argentina from taking the Falklands.
    b.   Egypt from taking the Suez Canal.
    c.   China from taking Hong Kong.
    d.   India from attacking Pakistan.
    e.   Serbs from killing Bosnians in Kosovo.

8. The European Community remains today

    a.   too weak to have any real effect on world affairs.
    b.   limited to former NATO Allies.
    c.   an organization dominated by Germany and France.
    d.   an economic but not a political union.
    e.   economically inferior to the United States and Japan.

9. President Richard Nixon resigned the U.S. presidency because

    a.   longtime opponents finally found enough corruption to impeach him.
    b.   he planned and oversaw a break-in at the Democratic headquarters.
    c.   he lied about his attempts to cover up the break-in.
    d.   his attempts at détente with the Russians were rejected by Congress.
    e.   the war in Vietnam proved to be out of control.

10. Despite being one of the world's most peaceful and progressive nations, Canada

    a.   feels controlled by its stronger neighbor, the United States.
    b.   continues to be plagued by separatist sentiments in Quebec.
    c.   has not been able to stem the tide of illegal aliens.
    d.   does not have enough natural resources to be a member of the G-8.
    e.   is home to one of the most dangerous nuclear plants in the world.

11. Name the group below that was not a terrorist organization of the 1970s and 1980s.

    a.   German's Baader-Meinhof Gang.
    b.   Belgium's Celtic Guard.
    c.   Italy's Red Brigades.
    d.   Northern Ireland's I.R.A.
    e.   France's Charles Martel Club.

12. Feminists after 1960 were most successful in

    a.   gaining spots on formerly men-only sporting teams.
    b.   creating a unisex style of clothing.
    c.   legalizing contraception and abortion.
    d.   gaining "equal pay for equal work" for women.
    e.   achieving equality for third world women.

13. "Guest workers" in most Western European countries

    a.   were often recruited to staff essential jobs.
    b.   by 1980 probably numbered fifteen million.
    c.   were most often concentrated in urban areas.
    d.   found themselves the objects of anti-foreign violence.
    e.   all of the above

14. "Happenings" or works of art rooted in performance

    a.   may have grown out of Pollock's Action Painting.
    b.   are written to played before live audiences.
    c.   have been highly popular on television.
    d.   may have contributed to the fall of the communist system.
    e.   all of the above

15. The novel *One Hundred Years of Solitude*

    a.   became one of the most successful films of the 1990s.
    b.   is one of the best illustrations of the style called "magic realism."
    c.   brought international fame and a Nobel Prize to its Czech author.
    d.   describes the Russian people under communism.
    e.   received excellent reviews despite not selling well.

16. The works of Milan Kundera demonstrate

    a. the full potential of Action Painting.
    b. that oppression does not destroy the human spirit.
    c. recent European dependence on Asian and African art.
    d. how state support of the arts can be effectively managed.
    e. a nostalgia for the security of the old socialist regimes.

17. The serialist music of Olivier Messiaen

    a. grew out of the folk styles of his native Finland.
    b. gained the respect of critics but has been largely ignored by the public.
    c. is often mistakenly said to have influenced minimalism.
    d. avoids any sort of repetition.
    e. utilizes clear and recognizable tonalities.

18. Like many other modern American composers, Philip Glass moved easily

    a. in radical political circles.
    b. from town to town to find sponsors.
    c. from classical to popular music and back.
    d. across national boundaries to avoid paying taxes.
    e. to higher income without losing his peasant touch.

19. E.F. Schumacher's work emphasized

    a. the need for technology to be responsible for environment preservation.
    b. that the computer would revolutionize modern business.
    c. the necessity for governments to balance their budgets.
    d. the need to return to harmonics in music.
    e. that without religious values modern man has lost his moral compass.

20. The recent growth of NGOs shows that people at the turn of the twenty-first century are

    a. pessimistic about hopes for world peace.
    b. turning to grass roots organizations to solve problems.
    c. more interested in profits than in human rights or the environment.
    d. as personally pious as were their grandparents.
    e. no longer interested or involved in politics.

Complete the Following Sentences:

1. Poland's move from Communist rule to a free market economy was led by _____, a _____ movement directed by its president _____ _____.

2. In Czechoslovakia, the dissident group _____ _____ led the opposition to the Communist regime; and the first post-communist leader was a playwright _____ _____, who granted _____ to thirty thousand prisoners.

3. In the former Yugoslavia, Serbian efforts to rid Bosnia of Muslims, which they called _____ cleansing, revived memories of _____ atrocities during World War II; yet NATO forces did not strongly retaliate until _____ Bosnians had been killed.

4. At first greeted with euphoria, German reunification later brought high _____ and _____ and physical attacks on Germany's _____ population.

5. Margaret Thatcher's government in Britain broke the power of the British _____ _____ and attacked _____ with austerity measures. Her popularity soared with victory in the _____ War.

6. Terrorism reached its peak in Italy when in 1978 former premier _____ _____ was kidnapped and killed by the _____ _____.

7. Because he considered the Soviet Union an _____ _____, U.S. President Ronald Reagan proposed a Strategic Defense Initiative, nicknamed _____ _____ after a popular film.

8. The 1986 disaster at _____ in the Soviet Union made the world more aware of the _____ threat, and European Green Parties proclaimed 1987 as the Year of the _____.

9. The new friendship between the U.S. and Russia was tested in 1990 when Iraq invaded _____, precipitating the _____ _____ War.

10. The most successful minimalist composer was _____ _____, who showed that his style could be adapted to a full-scale _____ and whose _____ was used in a documentary film.

Place the Following in Chronological Order and Give Dates:

1. Helmut Kohl chosen Chancellor of West Germany   1.

2. Dissolution of the U.S.S.R.   2.

3. Francois Mitterrand elected President of France   3.

4. Reunification of Germany   4.

5. Margaret Thatcher becomes British Prime Minister   5.

6. Solidarity Movement emerges in Poland   6.

7. Mikhail Gorbachev comes to power in the U.S.S.R.   7.

Questions for Critical Thought

1. What was Mikhail Gorbachev's role in the final act of the Cold War? How would events have been different without him? How will future historians likely judge him?

2. What directions did the Eastern European nations take once Soviet control ended? Why did they react as they did? Why the differences in results?

3. What were the major successes and failures of the Western European democracies after 1970? What were their motivations for and successes in forming the European Community?

4. How did the feminist movement after World War II differ from its pre-war counterparts? Does it now seem at last to have found its true focus?

5. Explain how modern movements in the arts and philosophy reflect both the uncertainty and the courage to experiment of the recent decades.

6. How does contemporary religion, said to be in a period of revival, compare and contrast with its counterpart before World War II?

7. Why has the contemporary world seen such an increase in terrorism? What new forms has it taken? What effects will it likely have on the democracies?

8. Describe the new globalism. How and why did it develop? How does it relate to the technological and social concerns of our age? What might it achieve?

Analysis of Primary Source Documents

1. What does Mikhail Gorbachev say made him decide that a "restructuring" of the Soviet system was necessary? In what sense does he believe such restructuring is needed around the world?

2. Describe what Vaclav Havel calls the "contaminated moral environment." Who is to blame, and what is the solution? Is this analysis too simple? Why or why not?

3. Show how the two news reports from the former Yugoslavia reflect the brutalizing effects of continuing war. Can you determine from these reports which side is to blame for the war crimes?

4. What characteristics of the future British Prime Minister are evident in Margaret Thatcher's early entry into politics? Are her actions those of a feminist?

5. Given the violence aimed at foreigners living in Germany, to what extent does it appear the same racism that produced Nazism is still alive there? What would you suggest the German government do to solve the problem?

6. What is Pope John Paul II's way of achieving world peace? To what degree could his philosophy be accepted by one who does not necessarily share his Catholic faith?

7. What does E.F. Schumacher mean when he says that people are using their capital as if it were income? What is his solution? How practical is it?

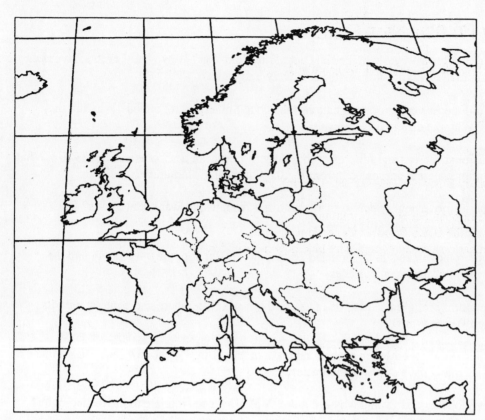

Map Exercise 17
Map A

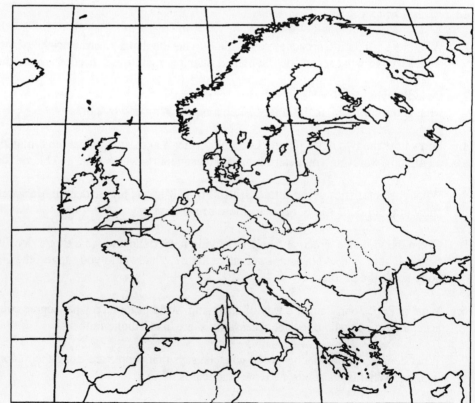

Map Exercise 17
Map B

MAP EXERCISE 17: THE NEW EUROPE

On Map A (The Cold War) shade and label the following:

1.   NATO bloc
2.   Warsaw Pact bloc
3.   Neutral nations
4.   Independent nations

On Map B (Contemporary Europe) shade and label the following:

1.   Members of the European Economic Community
2.   Former members of the U.S.S.R. now independent
3.   Eastern European nations, once in the Soviet bloc now independent

ANSWER KEY

CHAPTER 13

Matching

1. F
2. I
3. A
4. J
5. D
6. C
7. H
8. B
9. G
10. E

Multiple Choice

1. c
2. a
3. c
4. a
5. b
6. a
7. d
8. e
9. d
10. c
11. d
12. b
13. a
14. c
15. b
16. b
17. e
18. a
19. a
20. b

Completion

1. *Utopia*, divorce, Henry VIII
2. Augustinian, indulgences, Ninety-five
3. princes, peasants, gospel
4. Switzerland, Germany, Lord's Supper
5. Melchiorites, Münster, New Jerusalem
6. Catherine, Anne Boleyn, Edward VI
7. *Institutes of the Christian Religion*, sovereignty, predestination
8. wives, mothers, Eve
9. Huguenot, Catholic, France
10. Catholics, Mary, beheaded

Chronology

1. Diet of Worms: 1521
2. Schmalkaldic League formed: 1531
3. English Act of Supremacy: 1534
4. Calvin's *Institutes* published: 1536
5. Society of Jesus recognized: 1540
6. Council of Trent convenes: 1545
7. Spanish Armada: 1588

CHAPTER 14

Matching

1. B
2. J
3. E
4. C
5. I
6. H
7. F
8. D
9. A
10. G

Multiple Choice

1. d
2. b
3. b
4. c
5. e
6. a
7. c
8. b
9. c
10. d
11. a
12. b
13. a
14. c
15. d
16. b
17. a
18. c
19. b
20. c

Completion

1. navigator, Vasco da Gama, de Albuquerque
2. Hernán Cortés, Francesco Pizarro, de Las Casas
3. Laborers, protect, spiritual
4. 300, 450, 100, 10
5. Bengal, 3,000, Plassey
6. Macartney, Canton, Qianlong
7. missionaries, Nagasaki, three
8. legislatures, resented, resisted
9. unchangeable, war, expense
10. cattle, cane sugar, maize

Chronology

1. Dias around Africa: 1488
2. Tordesillas: 1494
3. First slaves to America: 1518
4. Champlain in Quebec: 1608
5. Dutch seize Malacca: 1641
6. Plassey: 1757
7. French cede Canada: 1763

CHAPTER 15

Matching

1. J
2. H
3. G
4. C
5. B
6. E
7. A
8. D
9. I
10. F

Multiple Choice

1. d
2. b
3. d
4. c
5. a
6. b
7. c
8. a
9. b
10. a
11. d
12. c
13. a
14. a
15. b
16. a
17. c
18. b
19. d
20. c

Completion

1. Nantes, Fontainebleau
2. finances, mercantilism, export, import
3. grandson, Spanish Succession
4. Frederick William, standing army, Commissariat
5. inquisition, Index, Jesuits
6. western, backward, technology
7. Catholic, Orange, Mary
8. constitutional, law, rights
9. commerce, Rembrandt, materialistic
10. *Tartuffe*, clergy, five

Chronology

1. Michael Romanov begins reign: 1613
2. *Leviathan* published: 1651
3. Turkish siege of Vienna: 1683
4. Edict of Fontainebleau: 1685
5. England's Glorious Revolution: 1688
6. Peter Romanov's trip to the West: 1697-98
7. War of Spanish Succession: 1702-1713

CHAPTER 16

Matching

1. H
2. D
3. A
4. J
5. G
6. B
7. C
8. I
9. E
10. F

Completion

1. Aristotle, Galen, Ptolemy
2. geometrizes, mathematical, Hermetic
3. Geocentric, Heliocentric, complicated
4. mountains, moons, sun
5. Simplicio, Sagredo, Salviati
6. calculus, light, gravity
7. liver, veins, arteries
8. mind, material world, Dualism
9. synagogue, panentheist, God
10. Charles II, Louis XIV, practical

Multiple Choice

1. d
2. a
3. b
4. e
5. d
6. a
7. a
8. b
9. a
10. c
11. c
12. c
13. e
14. a
15. b
16. c
17. b
18. b
19. d
20. d

Chronology

1. Copernicus' *Revolutions*: 1543
2. Galileo's *Messenger*: 1610
3. Bacon's *Instauration*: 1620
4. Harvey's *Motion*: 1628
5. Descartes' *Method*: 1637
6. Pascal's *Pensées*: 1669
7. Newton's *Principia*: 1687

CHAPTER 17

Matching

1. E
2. D
3. I
4. G
5. A
6. J
7. B
8. C
9. F
10. H

Multiple Choice

1. a
2. b
3. a
4. e
5. a
6. c
7. d
8. b
9. b
10. c
11. d
12. c
13. a
14. c
15. b
16. c
17. e
18. c
19. d
20. b

Completion

1. *Dictionary*, religious, heroes, David
2. Catholic Church, monarchy, checks, balances
3. deism, Jean Calas, murder, son
4. *Encyclopedia*, independence, revolt
5. mercantilism, agriculture
6. *Social Contract*, *Emile*, private property
7. aristocratic, Vierzehnheiligen
8. *Messiah*, *Don Giovanni*
9. Louis XIV, Roman Empire
10. education, Portugal, Spain, France

Chronology

1. Montesquieu's *Persian Letters*: 1721
2. Voltaire's *Philosophic Letters*: 1733
3. Diderot's *Encyclopedia* begun: 1751
4. Rousseau's *Social Contract*: 1762
5. Smith's *Wealth of Nations*: 1776
6. Gibbon's *Decline* completed: 1788
7. Condorcet's *Progress*: 1794

CHAPTER 18

Matching

1. D
2. I
3. J
4. G
5. A
6. E
7. B
8. H
9. C
10. F

Multiple Choice

1. d
2. e
3. b
4. b
5. d
6. a
7. d
8. c
9. a
10. c
11. d
12. b
13. c
14. c
15. c
16. b
17. d
18. a
19. b
20. c

Completion

1. pocket, landed gentry
2. George III, French, Napoleon
3. Voltaire, speech, press, toleration
4. Maria Theresa, Philosophy
5. Emelyan Pugachev, executed, agrarian reform
6. 30, 50, Two
7. India, North America, empire
8. wet nurses, clothes, toys
9. hoe, loose, drill
10. sophisticated, art, women

Chronology

1. Hanoverian succession: 1714
2. Frederick the Great begins reign: 1740
3. Seven Years' War: 1756-63
4. First Polish partition: 1772
5. Louis XVI begins reign: 1774
6. Joseph II begins reign: 1780
7. Retirement of Pitt the Younger: 1801

CHAPTER 19

Matching

1. J
2. A
3. G
4. B
5. D
6. C
7. H
8. F
9. I
10. E

Multiple Choice

1. a
2. c
3. c
4. b
5. b
6. d
7. c
8. e
9. a
10. a
11. b
12. d
13. b
14. c
15. e
16. a
17. c
18. a
19. b
20. d

Completion

1. robe, sword, monarchy
2. merchants, industrialists, bankers, land
3. financial, Versailles, Revolution
4. people, state, bishops
5. Girondin, Mountain, Mountain
6. Saint, Notre Dame, marry
7. Brumaire, Germinal, Fructidor
8. virtue, guillotine, radical
9. Egypt, abandoned, Paris
10. Elba, Waterloo, St. Helena

Chronology

1. Declaration of Independence: 1776
2. Storming of the Bastille: 1789
3. American Bill of Rights: 1791
4. Louis XVI executed: 1793
5. Napoleon's coronation: 1804
6. Continental System: 1806
7. Battle of Waterloo: 1815

CHAPTER 20

Matching

1. D
2. E
3. H
4. A
5. F
6. I
7. G
8. B
9. C
10. J

Multiple Choice

1. c
2. b
3. a
4. d
5. b
6. a
7. d
8. e
9. b
10. b
11. c
12. d
13. a
14. b
15. c
16. d
17. b
18. c
19. b
20. e

Completion

1. coal, iron, rivers, size
2. Arkwright, Cartwright
3. locomotive, *Rocket*
4. Crystal Palace, Kensington, Britain
5. coal, Ruhr, Rhineland
6. Catholic, Protestant, potato, starvation
7. Poor Law, atmospheric, sanitation
8. size, broken, cheap
9. males, paid, annually
10. twelve, nine, reading, arithmetic

Chronology

1. Watt's rotary steam engine: 1782
2. Cartwright's power loom: 1787
3. Trevithick's steam locomotive: 1804
4. Luddite attacks: 1812
5. People's Charter: 1838
6. Ten Hours Act: 1847
7. Great Exhibition: 1851

CHAPTER 21

Matching

1. D
2. H
3. A
4. J
5. F
6. B
7. I
8. C
9. G
10. E

Multiple Choice

1. b
2. c
3. a
4. c
5. d
6. e
7. a
8. d
9. b
10. b
11. c
12. a
13. d
14. c
15. a
16. c
17. c
18. d
19. b
20. a

Completion

1. Metternich, legitimacy, balance
2. Simón Bolivar, Monroe Doctrine
3. Russia, France, Britain, independent
4. Decembrist Revolt, Political Police
5. Thomas Malthus, David Ricardo
6. phalansteries, New Lanark, New Harmony
7. feminism, absolute equality
8. Louis-Philippe, Louis Napoleon Bonaparte
9. Debelleyme, *serjents*, cane, saber
10. Walter Scott, Mary Shelley

Chronology

1. Wars of Independence in Latin America begin: 1819
2. Greek revolt against the Turks begins: 1821
3. Decembrist Revolt in Russia: 1825
4. July Revolution in France: 1830
5. British Reform Act: 1832
6. Repeal of Corn Laws in Britain: 1846
7. Revolts or revolutions in France, Germany, Italy, and Austria: 1848

CHAPTER 22

Matching

1. E
2. H
3. A
4. J
5. B
6. F
7. I
8. D
9. C
10. G

Multiple Choice

1. a
2. e
3. d
4. c
5. d
6. a
7. b
8. e
9. b
10. a
11. d
12. b
13. a
14. c
15. b
16. a
17. a
18. b
19. c
20. d

Completion

1. Ottoman, Crimean, Britain, Concert
2. *Risorgimento*, Victor Emmanuel II, Savoy
3. Denmark, Austria, France, Empire
4. land, marry, assassination
5. Benjamin Disraeli, Liberal
6. Jewish rabbis, Protestant, atheism
7. *Communist Manifesto*, proletariat, bourgeoisie, classless
8. special, natural selection
9. romantic, adultery, suicide
10. German, Nibelung, epic

Chronology

1. Second French Empire proclaimed: 1852
2. Russian Emancipation Edict: 1861
3. American Civil War ends: 1865
4. Austro-Prussian War: 1866
5. British Reform Act: 1867
6. Italy annexes Rome: 1870
7. German Empire proclaimed: 1871

CHAPTER 23

Matching

1. F
2. I
3. C
4. E
5. A
6. H
7. B
8. J
9. D
10. G

Multiple Choice

1. a
2. c
3. a
4. d
5. c
6. a
7. b
8. e
9. d
10. c
11. a
12. b
13. c
14. b
15. d
16. a
17. c
18. e
19. b
20. c

Completion

1. German, Innovations, technical
2. white collar, teaching, nursing
3. Marxist, French revolution
4. 21, 147, 40, 80
5. London, Liverpool, private enterprise
6. condoms, diaphragms, infanticide
7. moral, civic, secular
8. commune, shot, penal colony
9. junker, monarchy, aristocracy, emperor
10. secret police, martial law

Chronology

1. Paris Commune: 1871
2. Spanish constitution: 1875
3. Bismarck's antisocialist law: 1878
4. Jacob's Clinic: 1882
5. British Housing Act: 1890
6. Nicholas II: 1894
7. Bernstein's *Socialism* published: 1899

CHAPTER 24

Matching

1. G
2. I
3. D
4. F
5. E
6. H
7. A
8. J
9. B
10. C

Multiple Choice

1. a
2. b
3. c
4. a
5. e
6. d
7. c
8. c
9. d
10. b
11. b
12. c
13. d
14. a
15. b
16. c
17. c
18. d
19. e
20. a

Completion

1. quanta, atoms, Isaac Newton
2. relativity, observer, time, space
3. unconscious, oblivious, dreams
4. Darwinism, war, biological
5. property, capitalism, socialism, Marxism
6. impression, light, modern
7. Asia, Africa, humanitarian, imperialism
8. Transvaal, Orange Free State, British
9. Boxers, Sun Yat-sen, Manchu
10. Meiji, Chinese, Korea, Russia

Chronology

1. British take Hong Kong: 1842
2. Suez Canal: 1869
3. Three Emperors' League: 1873
4. Victoria crowned Empress: 1876
5. Boxer Rebellion in China: 1900-1901
6. Triple Entente: 1907
7. Japan annexes Korea: 1910

CHAPTER 25

Matching

1. J
2. D
3. G
4. A
5. I
6. B
7. E
8. C
9. H
10. F

Multiple Choice

1. a
2. c
3. b
4. b
5. a
6. c
7. d
8. b
9. a
10. b
11. e
12. c
13. c
14. a
15. b
16. d
17. d
18. a
19. b
20. d

Completion

1. Irish, Poles, Slavs
2. Bosnian, Serbian, Black Head
3. Joffre, Marne, trench
4. Verdun, Somme, Champagne
5. shell, salary, explodes
6. submarine warfare, psychological
7. Hindenburg, Ludendorff, total war
8. Prime Minister, class
9. provisional, Bolsheviks, Lenin
10. Fourteen Points, Britain, France

Chronology

1. Francis Ferdinand assassinated: June, 1914
2. World War I begins: August, 1914
3. U.S. enters the war: April, 1917
4. Treaty of Brest-Litovsk: March, 1918
5. Second Battle of Marne: July, 1918
6. Armistice: November, 1918
7. Paris Conference begins: January, 1919

CHAPTER 26

Matching

1. G
2. I
3. B
4. J
5. A
6. C
7. H
8. D
9. E
10. F

Multiple Choice

1. c
2. a
3. b
4. c
5. e
6. b
7. c
8. b
9. d
10. b
11. c
12. a
13. b
14. a
15. d
16. d
17. c
18. b
19. c
20. a

Completion

1. League, Nations, France, Germany
2. reparations, Ruhr, inflation
3. demand, public works, deficit spending
4. working, New Deal
5. elementary school, *Avanti*, Fascist
6. Jews, Heinrich Himmler, *Hitler Jugend*
7. Bolsheviks, Leon Trotsky, Mexico
8. *Dopolavoro*, *Kraft durch Freude*
9. purposelessness, anti-art, Surrealist, unconscious
10. *Ulysses*, consciousness, Dublin

Chronology

1. Fascist dictatorship established in Italy: 1925
2. Stalin dictatorship established in Russia: 1929
3. National Government established in Britain: 1931
4. New Deal begun in the U.S.: 1933
5. Hitler dictatorship established in Germany: 1934
6. Popular Front formed in France: 1936
7. *Kristallnacht*: 1938

CHAPTER 27

Matching

1. J
2. D
3. B
4. F
5. H
6. A
7. I
8. C
9. G
10. E

Multiple Choice

1. e
2. b
3. d
4. c
5. a
6. b
7. e
8. a
9. c
10. b
11. c
12. a
13. c
14. d
15. c
16. a
17. b
18. d
19. c
20. d

Completion

1. Rhineland, Austria, Sudetenland
2. appeasement, Czechoslovakia
3. Poland, *blitzkrieg*, France
4. Pétain, puppet, Vichy
5. China, Indochina, Pearl Harbor
6. North Africa, Stalingrad, Coral Sea
7. Communists, Rose, Gestapo
8. Madagascar, Reinhard Heydrich, annihilation
9. Soviet Russia, Night Witches
10. American, Hiroshima, Nagasaki

Chronology

1. Occupation of Rhineland: March 7, 1936
2. Invasion of Poland: September 1, 1939
3. Battle of Britain: Fall, 1940
4. Attack on Pearl Harbor: December 7, 1941
5. Surrender at Stalingrad: February 2, 1943
6. Allied invasion of France: June 6, 1944
7. Atomic bomb on Hiroshima: August 6, 1945

CHAPTER 28

Matching

1. D
2. I
3. G
4. A
5. C
6. B
7. E
8. J
9. F
10. H

Multiple Choice

1. a
2. b
3. d
4. b
5. c
6. b
7. c
8. e
9. a
10. c
11. c
12. a
13. b
14. d
15. b
16. e
17. c
18. b
19. d
20. e

Completion

1. British, Greece, Turkey
2. Soviet, *Foreign Affairs*, containment
3. missiles, blockade, invade
4. Mao Zedong, private farmlands, industry, commerce
5. Stalin, satellites, Hungary, Czechoslovakia
6. Hungary, Red Army, Budapest
7. NATO, nuclear, automobiles, armaments
8. Economic miracle, Konrad Adenauer
9. bank, Insurance, Health
10. six, Rome, free trade zone

Chronology

1. Truman Doctrine: 1947
2. Formation of NATO: 1949
3. Formation of the Warsaw Pact: 1955
4. De Gaulle assumes power: 1958
5. Berlin Wall: 1961
6. Cuban Missile Crisis: 1962
7. Prague Spring: 1968

CHAPTER 29

Matching

1. J
2. D
3. G
4. A
5. I
6. B
7. H
8. C
9. F
10. E

Multiple Choice

1. b
2. c
3. e
4. d
5. c
6. b
7. a
8. d
9. c
10. b
11. b
12. c
13. e
14. a
15. b
16. b
17. b
18. c
19. a
20. b

Completion

1. Solidarity, labor, Lech Walesa
2. Civil Forum, Vaclav Havel, amnesty
3. ethnic, Nazi, 250,000
4. unemployment, taxes, foreign
5. labor unions, inflation, Falklands
6. Aldo Moro, Red Brigades
7. Evil Empire, Star Wars
8. Chernobyl, nuclear, Environment
9. Kuwait, Persian Gulf
10. Philip Glass, opera, *Koyaanisquatsi*

Chronology

1. Thatcher becomes British Prime Minister: 1979
2. Solidarity Movement emerges in Poland: 1980
3. Mitterrand elected President of France: 1981
4. Kohl chosen Chancellor of West Germany: 1982
5. Gorbachev comes to power in U.S.S.R.: 1985
6. Reunification of Germany: 1990
7. Dissolution of U.S.S.R.: 1992